Both Ends of the Rainbow

Lomilomi ~ A Healing Journey

Written by Gloria Ku'uleialoha Coppola

Foreword by Aunty Pualani Gillespie

Balboa Press books may be ordered through booksellers or by contacting:

Balboa Press
A Division of Hay House
1663 Liberty Drive
Bloomington, IN 47403
www.balboapress.com
1-(877) 407-4847

Because of the dynamic nature of the Internet, any web addresses or links contained in
this book may have changed since publication and may no longer be valid. The views
expressed in this work are solely those of the author and do not necessarily reflect the views
of the publisher, and the publisher hereby disclaims any responsibility for them.

The author of this book does not dispense medical advice or prescribe the use of any
technique as a form of treatment for physical, emotional, or medical problems without the
advice of a physician, either directly or indirectly. The intent of the author is only to offer
information of a general nature to help you in your quest for emotional and spiritual well-
being. In the event you use any of the information in this book for yourself, which is your
constitutional right, the author and the publisher assume no responsibility for your actions.

Certain stock imagery © Thinkstock.
Any people depicted in stock imagery provided by Thinkstock are models,
and such images are being used for illustrative purposes only.

ISBN: 978-1-4525-7412-7 (sc)
ISBN: 978-1-4525-7413-4 (e)

Library of Congress Control Number: 2013908337

Printed in the United States of America.

Balboa Press rev. date: 5/16/2013

~ *Dedication* ~

This book is dedicated to my entire ʻ*ohana* for all the love, support and encouragement throughout the years I have received. Without your unconditional love for me, I would not have been able to explore the world, heal my heart and be of service to mankind.

I also want to dedicate it to my grandchildren, the future generation who will pass on this knowledge so their lives may be in more balance.

I want to thank Dr. Samuel Schenker, my former employer who was the first one to introduce holistic health to me many years ago. We learned, explored, and brought healing to his neurology practice. It was here I learned about a system that would change my life and bring me to the massage profession.

I give immense gratitude to Candy Thomen, graphic designer and amazing colleague. Without her this book would not have been completed so beautifully!

To all my mentors in life, our journey together has helped me become the woman I am today who continually seeks a path of grace and harmony.

I give thanks to the islands of Hawaiʻi that have helped me heal.

I give thanks to Alita Thomas and Kate Hudak who diligently assisted with edits, along with many other colleagues that provided their eyes and feedback.

To every *kumu* that contributed their beautiful loving stories of lomi, I honor your aloha. You have taught me so much that I have applied in my life and share with my *haumana*.

To all the seen and unseen miracles that allowed this story to unfold.

~ *Acknowledgements* ~

As I journey down this path of healing I feel blessed to have owned a massage school, holistic center, health food store and now be involved with a divinely guided non-profit mission for massage therapists.

I acknowledge every teacher in my life, my parents, siblings, children, friends, mentors, neighbors and students. I thank Auntie Margaret Machado for being the first Hawaiian to offer her love and compassion to teach others the art of lomilomi. There are many who have shared different styles of lomi and their love with me.

I thank Kahu Abraham for sharing his wisdom to others so that I, too might learn from my Kumu Penny Prior and Ku'uipo Patricia Latonio.

I give thanks to Kumu Brenda Mohalapua Ignacio for teaching me about *pono* and for the gift of my Hawaiian name, Ku'uleialoha "My child of God's Love"

I also have much gratitude for the other Hawaiian *kumu* that have shared their love for the Hawaiian healing arts, including Kumu Karen Leialoha Carroll, Harry Uhane Jim, Kahu Leilani Kaleiohi, Aunty Angeline Locey and her son Michael Locey, Dane Silva and Pua Gillespie to name a few.

I feel most blessed for my 2 children, 4 grandchildren, my dog named Lomi, family, friends and my students. I was graced to bear witness of the birth of my daughter's first born son. Truly no present can be greater than this gift.

While listening to divine guidance I have created the Aloha Message cards with the assistance of one of my students who is also a graphic artist and friend who is helping me with this book. As well, thank you Candy L. Thomen.

And because you are reading this now, I have followed yet more guidance to complete this book in its time as ke Akua/Creator/God has so summoned. Thank you God.

CONTENTS

Preface

"In order to relate to the community and to society as a whole in a meaningful way, one must be selfless and conscious of the silent workings of nature through every living thing."

~ *Virginia Burden*

The history of lomilomi is not easy to trace as nothing was ever in written word. Healing techniques and tools were handed down in an oral tradition to each ʻohana.

In this book you will learn about some of the teachers who have brought this healing art to non-Hawaiians. I hope that you will gain a greater understanding and respect for the meaning of Aloha. I will share how your life's purpose is always speaking to you, if you pay attention. You will learn how to create balance in your life through the teachings of Lokahi and live a life of lomi. You will find a great diversity from each family and between the islands, as well.

As Kumu Karen will share Healing with Shells, others will share their gifts handed down to them by their family.

Each practitioner is different, however the foundation is prayer and love. I have learned through my studies there may be differences of opinions or ideas but there is never a disagreement on the foundation. I have also read "All wisdom is not taught in one school".

On my visit to the Bishop Museum on Oahu I did not find any historical information on lomilomi; however I found so much on their culture, which is the lomi lifestyle. This includes the herbal remedies, honoring each day and paying reverence to all that *ke Akua* (Creator) has given us. They honor the earth and it's cycles of life.

I have learned that after the missionary's came to the islands, many hid in the valleys, left the islands, while others were slaughtered. Much of the history was lost during this time as well as the use of the Hawaiian language.

When the Hawaiians came back to their islands they brought information, wisdom and tools from Asia, Europe and Indonesia. I can see the integration of these forms of healing in lomilomi. Today, there is a re-emergence of this culture and it is touching the hearts of all those open to receive this wisdom. It is a beautiful way of life that can create harmony on this planet.

It is my intention to share my healing journey through lomilomi and give respect to all those that share their love for this ancient healing art and lifestyle. Aunty Margaret Machado played a significant role in passing on this healing touch to the non-hawaiians.

This is not a manual to teach you lomilomi; it is a guide with contributions from several kumu and my healing journey. There are some illustrations of techniques I will provide so that you can get a sense of the variety of techniques and styles that are taught.

In humble gratitude for what I have learned on my healing journey. I share with you through my eyes of Aloha.

Mahalo ke Akua, for blessings great and small.
Mahalo ke Akua, your great love touches all.
Let us be mirrors of your light, keepers of your love.
Mahalo ke Akua for your blessings from above.
We ask for your protection and blessings,
from the top of our head to the souls of our feet
and the four corners of our body
and wherever it is needed to go.

Loving-kindness Meditation

May the hearts of all beings be filled with happiness
and peace
(free from suffering and distress)

May all beings be safe and secure
(free from fear and harm)

May all beings be healthy and prosperous
(free from pain, illness and lack)

May all beings live joyfully and with ease
(free from struggle and conflict)

~Buddha Shakyamuni

FOREWORD

Dedicated to Aunty Margaret Machado,
the first Hawaiian to share lomilomi with non-Hawaiians

~ *"Kealaola" The Pathway to Healing* ~

The warm sun against my skin as I left the plane at Kona International airport was a blessing after flying for 6 hours. The light fragrance of plumeria and fresh ocean air came over me and I knew I was home. Exhausted, but excited to be on my new adventure, I was able to maneuver my four-legged aluminum companion, otherwise known as my walker, out to the curb to await a taxi. I had only my backpack because I wasn't going to stay long, I thought, and enough clothes for a week of relaxation on the Big Island of Hawaii.

I had been coming to Kealakekua Bay as a child to spend time with my *'ohana* (family) every summer so I knew how to get to the little village of Napo'opo'o, but never had been to the famous beach house of Aunty Margaret Machado and her Lomilomi classes. My *makuahine* (mother) had taken me to meet Aunty Margaret in 1981, after my mom was diagnosed with terminal lung cancer. The oncologists had told my mom to make final preparations for her end of life and

Aunty Margaret's beach house in Napo'opo'o

she told me that she was going to try a little Hawaiian healing to help her with her journey.

We visited Aunty Margaret at her office in the village of Kealakekua, where I met this smiling woman dressed in a white nurse's uniform and she had a distinct *'imo'imo* or sparkle in her eye. My mom spent two hours with Aunty and when she returned to us there was a calming peace surrounding her. Her gentle countenance was so different than I had ever experienced with my mom. She said "This is exactly what I needed to move on" and that Aunty had shown her a *kealaola* or pathway to healing. My mom passed away six months later but she had never been more happy, smiling and peaceful as she approached the end of this journey. She stated to me that one day I would need Aunty's prayer and loving touch and I also would be blessed with a journey of healing. My mother's eyes had that same *'imo'imo* in her gaze upon me as she transitioned to eternity.

Little did I know that my journey would begin as I awaited a taxi at the airport. I had been in a tragic auto accident three years earlier which left me in a wheelchair and only able to walk a few steps with the assistance of a caregiver and a walker. I had succumbed to a world of negativity, severe depression and prescription pain medicine addiction. A small quiet voice kept encouraging me to return to my roots and find my path. My stubborn Western Medicine background put little faith in alternative therapies, prayer and forgiveness as a way to healing my body and mind.

The taxi took 55 minutes to get to my intended destination and suddenly stopped in front of a long lava dirt road filled with 6 inch pot holes and stained streaks of transmission oil on the ground. "You're going to have to walk from here because I am not allowed to take my taxi down this road. You will find where you are going at the end of the road about ¼ mile." I looked at the man like he was cruel and crazy, but I had no choice but to begin to walk down this road. Walker and backpack and a good bottle of water, I began this journey in the hot sun of a Hawaiian afternoon with rainclouds looming overhead. I would walk about 25 steps and then sit, then continue on 25 more. With each step I felt stronger yet my mind was filled with negative and self-abasing thoughts regarding how crazy I was to do this unknown and unproven treatment.

After 1 hour of walking I approached the tiny fishing village of Ke`ei and suddenly I could see a figure in the distance waving to me and calling for me to come. She was dressed in a flowery mu`u-mu`u and had three plumerias in her hair. As I approached her, grasped her welcoming hand, the peace and serenity of knowing I made the right decision came upon me. I suddenly knew I was at the right place and at the right time. She had just made some lunch of good vegetables and rice as well as some fresh fruit for dessert. It was the best meal I had tasted in a long time. We ate out in the yard and she shared with me that I was to stay at this beach house and begin to change my life. It was the love of God that was going to heal me and with daily prayer I was going to get through this ordeal. She looked at my "aluminum companion" and said when you leave here "you will wish this friend a fond aloha". We prayed together and I spent the afternoon sleeping in the back area of her beach house called the "Aloha Suite". This area was reserved for students who were arriving the following week for classes in Lomilomi massage and Hawaiian herbal medicine called *lāʻau lapaʻau*. I would be part of this class as a demonstration model and they would work on me daily, learning about Lomilomi, prayer and forgiveness. My first mission was to detox from the heavy pain medication and we did this in small doses mixed with prayer, massage and steambaths to help cleanse my body and we used a flowering herb to help cleanse and regenerate my liver from three years of opiate based pain medication.

The students were so kind and eager to work on my body and we used the 12 steps of the front porch of the beach house as a tool to build strength in the muscles of my hips and legs. Every morning would begin with a wonderful song "My God and I go in the Field Together" and end with "God's Love is Like a Circle" followed by a steam bath and swimming in the ocean. I remember Aunty's singing voice as they massaged me using sweet sounding names for massage strokes like "Wiggly-Wiggly", Hawaiian Poi Pounder and the waltz like 1-2-3 and 1-2-3 as she would count out the rhythm of this magical massage. The students would help me go to the ocean and aid me to float in the gentle waves of the greatest healing medium of all, seawater. Every day we would learn about the human body and Aunty would share stories of past students and patients that were stories of miracles that would happen on the very porch upon which we were sitting. Little did I know that one day students would be hearing of my journey and the healing that took place during my stay.

Aunty would always share the importance of her three basic principles of living Lomilomi. Lomilomi is a work of prayer, forgiveness and unconditional love. To walk this path and to be a true practitioner of this work, we must strive to live in these three graces each day. Prayer aligns your communication with God.

Aunty's lifelong background was in the 7th Day Adventist faith and so her prayers were Christian based but she never judged or evangelized anyone who came to her for healing or education. Her message was for all faiths, cultural beliefs and all people. Aunty Margaret would always look for the good in each person and never speak of negative influences that encounter us on a daily basis. Aunty always taught that you must be free of any negativity, hurt feelings and bitter thoughts before falling asleep each night.

"You cannot go to sleep with a troubled mind or an unforgiving heart for these will cause negative changes to the muscles, nerves and blood vessels and will lead to chronic disease, broken relationships and family troubles."

"You must go to the ocean and ask God to help you to forgive others who have offended you and forgive yourself if you have offended anyone."

Walking in this path may be challenging but we must always continue to forgive each other and ourselves to bring inner peace and make room for unconditional love.

Walking in the unconditional love of Aloha is a Hawaiian concept that has been taught by many and followed by few. Aunty Margaret was the true spirit of Aloha. She lived in unconditional love for all. She helped anyone who came to her and always walked in forgiveness. When someone had a problem or concern, she always focused them on the positive aspects of the situation and helped them to find a solution that always reflected love and forgiveness. We would have numerous students over the years that were very troubled from broken relationships, family abuse, substance addiction and she never rejected anyone from receiving her care. For anyone who could not afford her classes, she would find them small jobs to do around the beach house or neighborhood so they could still earn their education respectfully.

Following my nine weeks with Aunty Margaret I was able to ceremoniously throw my "aluminum companion" into the ocean and continue down my path of healing, drug free, filled with forgiveness for all who offended me. I forgave the man who caused me to be in the wheelchair, and moved forward with my life, free from bitterness and filled with forgiveness.

I returned to that miraculous Beach house in 2001, now humbly honored as a teacher of Anatomical Science and would share Hawaiian Culture with weekend cultural tours with students from 7 continents, speaking numerous languages, and sharing diverse cultural experiences. Aunty Margaret and her husband and co-pilot Uncle Dan Machado would supervise as their daughter Nerita Machado and I were the teaching team for up to 12 students at a time. We always tried, with Aunty's guidance, to live the path of Lomilomi. Aunty would always share her wonderful stories, and share her most meaningful teachings:

"Touch the body with a loving touch.
If your hands are gentle and loving, your patient will feel the sincerity of your heart.
Their soul will reach out to yours and God's Healing will flow though you both."

"Your mind is your Garden; your thoughts are your seeds;
you can grow flowers or you can grow weeds"

"Lomilomi is a praying work. You are not the Healer; God is the healer!"

"Never let the sun go down on an angry heart.
Stand at the ocean and ask God for help to forgive"

Aunty Margaret and Pua
"Always walk in Pule, Ho`oponopono and Aloha. God will do the rest"

Pua Gillespie

I spent many meaningful years with Aunty and her family. We taught many students about the wonders of the body and the meanings of *pule*, *ho`oponopono* and *aloha*, and the miraculous healing of Hawaiian Lomilomi massage. We spent many nights listening to wonderful stories from students from all over the world who came to find their *kealaola*.

I was honored to be with Aunty Margaret and her family as she transitioned to eternity. She was peaceful, loving and so kind, until her very last breath with us. I know that her work continues in heaven where she is at the right hand of her beloved Jesus and she is surrounded by her loved ones.

My *kealaola* continues, just as my mother said it would, and today I still have that little *'imo'imo* in my eye. Mahalo Aunty Margaret for all you gave to us and you live on in our hearts of Aloha each day.

~ *Aunty Pua Gillespie*

Keepers of the Rainbow's Light
Kahu malama a ao ke ʻanuenue
~ Kuʻuleialoha

We welcome the keepers of the rainbows light

As haumana you will continue to learn about the secrets of healing

You must remember to leave your troubles
For they are no longer yours
Surrender them to ke Akua
They will be embraced and transmuted

Listen attentively each day for your message
Clear your mind and open your heart and remember to breathe

For the breath, you must remember is your ola
Ask yourself, How do I choose to live?

There is no more time to wander on this earth
Show up now
Listen to your calling, you have been chosen

Your kumu have given you all the wisdom you need to get started on your journey
It is your kuleana to open to the knowledge of the ʻAumakua now

Receive, allow yourself to receive Lomi

For herein lies the secrets to your desires
It cannot be found in a book or a class
It can only be found when you love yourself fully
Only then do you heal and help others to heal
Only then will you know what we speak of
Only then will the secrets be revealed

Wait no more
Breathe and accept now
You are blessed
E Komo Mai
Begin to walk your life in Pono

Introduction

Welcome to my story of a healing journey and how it brought me to lomilomi. Hawaiian healing would change my life.

Aloha Messages from Ku'uleialoha

I was born and raised in New York City by an Italian father and Polish mother. My parents weren't quite sure where my fascination for anything Hawaiian came from although they did appease me by gifting me with a hula doll one Christmas. You'd find my head in the movies that featured anything Hawaiian with Nancy Wu, Elvis Presley and Don Ho at a very young age. My eyes were mesmerized by the turquoise waters, my ears were filled with beautiful songs and my heart would feel the grace of the hula on depths I did not understand at such a young age either. If there is truly a past life, I am sure I have lived in Hawai'i many lifetimes.

I am telling you this story, because the Hawaiians teach through story telling. The ancestry is important as is every turn in our life events.

My dream was to be a doctor or a teacher one day. Oh and a singer and a dancer too. You will see how this life unfolds in my transformational journey.

I entered Hunter College in New York to pursue a medical field one day. I was excited when I was able to obtain a summer job in Bellevue Hospital working along with the handicapped children. It was during this summer that I also found out how much I loved helping those that seemed less fortunate than I. I was to learn not only from these amazing children, but others along my path that you can live in joy no matter what, if you so choose.

Shortly thereafter, I married and had two beautiful children, a boy and a girl. I loved waking up to their inquisitive minds and sparkling eyes each day. Redirecting my career was a little disappointing. However, my life would soon be filled with the joy of children. The years flew by quickly and along the way I continued to take classes in business and psychology, for I knew one day I would be doing something more to contribute to the world.

One day a heaviness came upon me. I wasn't feeling very fulfilled and my soul was screaming out loudly "What are you teaching your children?" It was in that very moment I knew a difficult decision would be made to move forward on my spiritual path. That meant I would leave my spouse, who at the time, did not seem to understand me. It was such a hard decision to make and something I never imagined, divorce.

So many changes came quickly. I had no idea where my life was leading but I knew I had to follow the energy and the intuition of my heart and soul.

At that time I was the business manager for a neurologist. It was during this time that my life was about to be led in another direction, one of healing. The physician came into my office one day and asked me to find out everything I could about holistic medicine. I had never even heard of holistic, however if you put me on a mission, you are sure to get results.

Soon I would be studying Iridology, homeopathy, herbology and aromatherapy. I attended a networking meeting to promote the neurological center and it was here I met the first massage therapist who was going to provide me with my first massage ever. I remember how intrigued I was experiencing the sensations in my body as her hands rubbed on my muscles. Within a few months I would find myself in massage school in the evenings, after a long day at work. I attended two massage schools, actually. I loved learning about the anatomy and physiology. I enjoyed experiencing all the new techniques. I was so inquisitive about the varieties of healing methods too.

I now had a life that included the healing arts and it would never be the same. Everything I was learning was amazing and I wanted to share my knowledge with anyone willing to learn. I opened a holistic health center in New Jersey. My practice grew quickly, despite a recession in the economy. I continued to attend more trainings. I studied all the levels of cranio-sacral therapy, neuromuscular therapy and myofascial release. My practice was booming.

I decided to offer a basic massage technique course in a community school to the general public. It was during this time three young women asked me if I would train them in massage. Obviously, I did not have a massage school, so I referred them to the one I attended in Princeton, New Jersey. A few minutes later, one of the young women came back over to me with her aunt.

*"Touch is such
an immediate
sense. It can
bring you in from
the false world.
Rediscovering
the sense of touch
returns you to the
heart of your own
spirit, enabling
you to experience
warmth, tenderness
and belonging...*

*Touch offers
the deepest clue
to the mystery
of encounter,
awakening and
belonging."*

*~ Anam Cara by John
O'Donohue*

This woman was a successful entrepreneur and in a stern and confident manner, she explained to me that opportunity was knocking on my door. She proceeded to express that I had just taught over 60 people successfully and that I would teach her niece. I was being divinely directed to open a massage school. Within a few months I was able to open the doors to an approved massage school. Although I did not know it at the time, everything was aligned in my life to bring me exactly to this moment so that you could also gain inspiration to follow your path.

My childhood dreams were manifesting. I had a full time massage practice helping others who wanted to heal their body, mind and spirit and I was passionately teaching all I was learning. I was a healing arts teacher for the next 12 years. I would continue to study Thai Yoga massage, Reiki, Myoskeletal alignment, Hot stones and so much more. I was a massage workshop junkie! Life was full, happy, healthy and thriving!

One day a client of mine noticed a man talking to me. "Who is he? Don't let that one get away" she said. I took another look and saw a remarkable spirit that was about to journey with me. I had no idea what that meant at the moment. This man would one day be my partner. We would work together, grow together and eventually marry. It was exciting to have someone who understood where you were coming from and shared mutual feelings, ideas and passion. Despite the bumps in the road all relationships go through we worked together beautifully. Together we would coordinate a Body, Mind, Spirit conference with another colleague. It was here that we would teach an amazing course on Relationships. I went on my first camping trip with him and loved it. I would come home after a long days work to roses aligned on the stairway all the way to my garden tub. Candles and soft music would welcome me home. Eventually, 3 years later we would celebrate our union and be married. In 1998, we moved into our new home just before the Christmas holiday. Life was great! My school was booming. My spouse was getting ready to graduate successfully as a psychologist. His personal challenges were his greatest obstacle and he was determined to release them. It was during the week prior to Christmas a tragic event was about to happen. Addicted to prescription pain killers, he attempted to rid himself of this unsuccessfully. My newly wedded spouse transitioned to the spirit world. I remained in shock for months and the depression grew heavier over the year. Surely this was not what was to be? I was angry and confused. No, I was MAD!

I was about to experience a connection with the spirit world far deeper than I imagined. There were messages and symbols and interventions almost daily. It was so overwhelming at times I did not know how to handle it. I would see visions and have intense dreams about my spouse. Items would appear by my side. He was telling me he was right there, watching over me. I would never be the same; I could assure you. I knew he was going to teach me many things from the spirit world.

Months upon months I lay in bed finding it difficult to do anything. Then an angel appeared in my life truly by divine intervention. This connection brought me to an island I did not even know existed; Kaua'i, the Garden Island. I packed up, sold my house and most of my possessions and left the pressures of running my massage school in the hands of others. I had no idea what would unfold; I just took the chance and listened to my guidance.

During the first two years on this magical island I stayed mainly to myself healing and learning about a connection with the 'āina (nature), something I had lost. I would wake up to the sunrise on my body and pray (*pule*) and ask "Am I really here?"

The fragrant smells of pikaki, plumeria and yellow ginger allured my senses. The sweet juice of lilikoi and tender coconuts, fresh sunrise papaya satiated my palate with gifts of the gods. The greatest medicine to heal depression was right within my senses. I was blessed as I walked the

O wau La'a Ao, O wau La'a Ao

I am the Sacred Light

O wau Aloha, O wau Aloha,

I am Love

O wau Mau Loa, O wau Mau Loa,

I am eternal

~ Elithe Manuha'aipo Kahn, PhD

"May we walk gently upon this earth and be in harmony with all creatures.

May we hold our hearts as gentle as we would the feather of an angel

in the palm of our hands . May we walk in gratitude"

~ Ku'uleialoha

white sandy beaches. I had gratitude for these sacred grounds and felt something good coming soon.

With almost three decades of my life focused on a path of healing, it is now that I was beginning to understand that everything was preparing me for an initiation deeper into my soul's journey. I was about to find out more than I imagined about my purpose in life. With this gift I would teach others the possibilities available to live a life of love and joy, Aloha.

I have explored many sacred places on this beautiful planet including Sedona, AZ; Cherokee, NC; Black Hills, SD; the Vancouver Islands, Peru; Egypt to name a few and now Hawai'i. My guides, mentors and angels walk with me each moment and when I fully show up with presence and heightened awareness, without resistance, I learned quickly that you can manifest things beyond your dreams very quickly.

While I do not make claims to be an expert in all that is Hawaiian and I am still learning so much, I feel my love and passion for the Hawaiian culture and healing arts is something that spirit has been guiding me to share with you. I am not Hawaiian in this lifetime, however, many Hawaiians have said to me and believe we are all connected in our DNA. In the Hawaiian healing video I show my students, a documentary by John C. Zak; Roland Cazimero, a musician, shares there are more non-Hawaiians that live Hawaiian.

I can claim that my life has revolved and evolved around a healing path and many of my mentors, including my ancestry, have prepared me well for living a life based in spiritual principles.

It is with deepest gratitude and respect that I thank all that have taught me in this life, from the beginning of time and before. I acknowledge your wisdom, devotion and honor the love you have for me on all levels.

My story now continues with a joyful enthusiasm to share more on lomilomi. My purpose in this lifetime is to share through teaching the depths of healing that I continue to learn.

CHAPTER ONE

~ *Lomilomi Finds Me* ~

"Dreaming of a life that is fulfilling and balanced where peace and love co-exist in harmony with nature and our creator" my definition of lomilomi.

Imagine sitting at a small smoothie stand, colorfully painted with yellows, pinks and greens on the island of Kaua'i. The wooden porch creaks on this bright sunny day with skies of vibrant blues as you sip a fresh fruit smoothie made with coconut, papaya, pineapple and passion fruit. Breathing the scents of the newly blossomed plumeria, it was here that lomilomi found me at Mango Mama's. I shall never forget this moment.

As I sat cherishing this peaceful moment I noticed a brochure on the bar top counter. There was something familiar about one of the photos. I recognized a woman from New Jersey, Ku'uipo Patricia Latanio. Many people had told me I must meet her and here she was, on the brochure. I picked it up and began to read the content. It was all about Hawaiian massage aka Lomilomi. This came at a time when I had no desire to take another class. I actually had told my staff I was never going to do massage or teach again when I left my massage school in New Jersey. I was not in a position to financially take a class at this time. I did have the time, 30 days required for this intensive training. Without hesitation, I put the one brochure back on the counter and continued to appreciate the sensations and flavors of my fresh fruit smoothie. Life was healing!

The next morning in my tiny studio apartment I awoke to another beautiful day. I was taking my shower when a voice spoke to me loudly and clearly. I was directed to take this Lomilomi course. I could not doubt another message from a higher source was guiding me. Off I went to Mango Mama's. I must admit, as I was driving there, I prayed the brochure was gone.

However, you guessed it, it was still there. I proceeded to dial the number on the brochure and Ku'uipo answered the call. Much to her surprise we had finally connected after many years of both of us hearing from mutual colleagues we needed to meet. We chatted for a while and I explained my situation. It was done.

Two days later I was driving to the YMCA camp at Waimea canyon for my 30-day residential training. I arrived at the top of the mountain with my old island style car when my brakes failed. I knew in that moment I was not getting out until it was time. I sat on the lawn, looked around at the old camp site and just laughed. As I unpacked and entered the cold bunk house, I had no idea what this training was going to entail. There were over 30 people including assistants finding their way, some excited some doubtful, some confused, and some not so happy we were in a co-ed bunk house.

Every day we woke up before the crack of dawn to do two hours of kundalini yoga and breathwork. Afterwards, we would share in a circle as long as was needed before breakfast was served. We had daily chores as part of creating community and being of service. We also learned martial art movements, the Flight, hula, feng shui, gestalt therapy, bioenergetics and ho'oponopono. It was quite a full day and we had not even touched a body.

Why no hands on? Traditionally, you were chosen by a *kahuna lomilomi* and you might spend up to thirty years studying together. Lomi is not only about the massage. There are many things that one must do as a practitioner and as a client before the body is ready to receive massage. This is the process. Our days included many things that did not involve massage, all as preparation for this life path.

As you might imagine, there were many emotions surfacing. We were learning about ourselves and how we move in this world with our bodies. We would explore where our *mana* (energy) was blocked, physically, emotionally, mentally and spiritually. Our days were long and often we did not go to bed until midnight. It was approximately on the 9th day when we were introduced to the hands on portion of the lomilomi massage techniques. We would now learn about the Ka Huna bodywork that Kahu Abraham Kawai'i taught his students. This type of lomilomi has also been called temple style lomi. This ancient healing system was handed down through the generations. They kept many things secret within their ʻohana (family). Many of the *kupuna* (elder) today still cherish these secrets within their Hawaiian families.

My story contains many journeys and challenging times and enlightening moments. The details are not important. The outcome is a fuller, richer, happier life and a reason to celebrate your spirit! I acknowledge that this healing system brought me to a greater understanding of life and healing. I will always cherish these lessons. The lomilomi training was not easy, it was life changing.

I will continue to represent the best I can, the inspiration and knowledge that was shared by many *kahuna* and *kumu* who taught me the true essence of Alo~HA, which is a life of Lomilomi.

*The flight was used to prepare the practitioner.
A form of martial art, lua, it would build your mana and shift levels of your consciousness.*

CHAPTER TWO

~ *What is lomilomi?* ~

"...healing is
a recovery of
wholeness or what
spiritual traditions
call enlightenment."

~ Amit Goswami,
PhD,
from his book
The Quantum Doctor

The most familiar and common description of Lomilomi is compassionate touch. However, I have learned that it is more, it is a lifestyle.

Lomilomi goes far beyond massage as I previously mentioned. It is a method of Hawaiian healing that is all encompassing to create *lōkahi* (balance, harmony and unity) in our life. Lomi reflects the connection with the *'āina* (nature) and the spirit of the ancestors (*'Aumakua*) as well as the breath (*hā*) and essence of our creator, *ke Akua*.

We learn in lomi how to live in balance and build our *mana* (spiritual energy). It is this *mana* that a lomi practitioner will use to nurture, to bless the cells and to bring balance to the client receiving this healing work.

TRAININGS

If you ever take or have taken a lomilomi training, please know this book is *only a guide.* You will learn lomi involves more than technique. It is a true healing art. When embarking upon the studies of this healing art, one must know that it is a journey of self discovery. A path of transformation. A life of service. It will take you a lifetime to implement it all.

All traditional lomilomi begins with *pule*, the power of prayer. Every practitioner learns how to create sacred space within oneself and their environment. There is gratitude given upon completion of a session not only to the client, but to the *'Aumakua* and *ke Akua*. Nothing is ever taken for granted and the healing messages are always received through the lomi practitioner as a blessing.

You might also read that some Hawaiians believe lomi should only be passed on by Hawaiians and for no profit. Some believe there is only one traditional style. With all the Hawaiian *kumu* I have met, I believe they are all coming from their *pu'uwai* (heart center) and sharing loving touch in a profound way. I feel those living in integrity to share this love are not exploiting lomilomi. I believe it is a time when this planet needs more love and understanding. I do not believe any one can claim rights for compassionate touch and that it comes from a source beyond ourselves through our heart and hands through *ke Akua*.

I have read that some don't feel most of Kahu Abraham's teachings are traditional and have made accusations of rituals that I have never personally witnessed or been a part of in my trainings. While this is disturbing to hear I want to assure those that pursue lomi they should make sure their teachers only represent this healing work from the heart (*pu'uwai*). My lineage includes the teachings of Kahu Abraham and Aunty Margaret. Two beautiful souls sharing the Aloha.

As lomi becomes more popular throughout the world we may find many styles and interpretations evolving. Some Hawaiians do not feel the 'western' version fully represents the traditional style of the true spiritual context. I can understand their concern and feelings about this ancient healing art being misinterpreted, washed down and exploited to some degree. I would like to add that in my opinion, lomilomi must be of a spiritual nature to touch the depths of this profound healing method. I do not personally feel a practitioner can be prepared in a weekend course and we must realize those types of trainings merely touch upon the essence of this work.

From my studies, experiences and readings lomilomi traditionally began with a detoxification process. Utilizing herbal medicine (*lā'au lapa'au*), Hawaiian salts, steam and *ho'oponopono* always preceded the actual massage, when needed. Lomilomi might also include learning how to read the energy, to breathe properly and to utilize the *hā* (breath) to move energy or clear blockages. You might also see techniques that resemble many of the oriental modalities, like

Hawaiian salt is used to rub and cleanse the body as a poultice for pain or as an exfoliant.

Often it is combined with 'alaea, the red earth containing hematite.

Thai massage for example. Thai includes many stretches and compressions along with joint movements very similarly performed in lomilomi sessions. There is an abundance of Asian influence on the islands, so one must remember each 'ohana integrates what was taught from their lineage. Deep tissue techniques are applied as well when the body is ready and prepared to receive. Often people think lomilomi is just a light massage, when in fact that is not truth. Lomilomi works on all states of our body from the etheric to the physical with different stages and amounts of pressure, depending on what the client is ready and willing to receive.

We also have to learn about heightened levels of awareness and practice opening these channels. We are taught to follow the body into the spaces ready to shift. Then it becomes easier for the practitioner to apply a technique that will feel deeper, because the client will be ready to receive. It is believed that as long as we remain an open clear vessel, wisdom will be provided by *ke Akua* to provide profound healing or shifting and will transform an individual as they transcend time and space.

All Hawaiian words have many meanings and many hidden meanings. One of the meanings of lomilomi can be found in *Wise Secrets of Aloha*, meaning *to shift*. We shift our being through the power of this healing touch. We shift our consciousness to the state of bliss, where there is unlimited possibilities to healing.

CHAPTER THREE

~ *The Lomilomi Experience* ~

The light that shines, the oneness we create through breath with all that is

~ *HĀ* ~

~ Ku'uleialoha from the Aloha Messages Cards

To truly understand lomilomi one must experience it by a skilled practitioner who lives lomi in their life on all levels.

As I recall my first true lomi experience, which was not in the training, the practitioner took time to create sacred space and clear himself and the room before *receiving* me. This took approximately one hour. Upon his first greeting and connection with me I already felt a shift. I knew something was different as the session began with beauty and grace. The chant *E Ho Mai* over my body was more powerful than anything I experienced as the *oli* (chant) came from the depths of his spirit as the earth vibrated through our core. I transcended time and space in that moment. The bliss I experienced was beyond anything I had previously felt as a massage instructor with a school and receiving thousands of massages from therapist and students over the course of my career. This healing session has no descriptive words. Everyone's experience will vary and each session will be different because we are always shifting. Depending on your openness to receive, you may experience different levels of healing. You may not even be consciously aware of them in that moment.

Lomi will change the way you feel, move, think and breathe. Healing is increased by love, given and received. This is the '*secret*' of Lomi. There has not been a lomi session that has felt the same to me and each experience has been what was needed in that moment. I am reminded, I get what I am willing to receive.

Several years ago I was privileged to receive a lomi at Aunty Angeline's by two wonderful and highly skilled lomi practitioners. Of course, as an instructor I wanted to learn, but soon realized I was being ridiculous paying attention to techniques. It is not about the technique. At the end of the session, I sat up. It was then I realized I was in a different space. I shifted without conscious thought. I shifted without knowing or realizing while the massage was being performed. Although I have never used recreational drugs, I would equate it to being high. For almost 6 hours I was floating and not fully integrated into the world as I once had known it. I would never be the same.

Kumu Michael Locey shared with me on Kaua'i why lomi is so special. "All things are sacred in Hawai'i. To us, that means feeling it, from your head to toe, above and below. Realizing the air we breathe is alive and a conductor of the source of life force. The words we use have recognition of our connection to the source of life as we chant our geneology, our intentions. *Kanaka Maoli* (native Hawaiian) literally means 'real man'. Our geneology links us to our ancestors ('*Aumakua*) and *kumu* (teachers). We become extensions of them in the divine breath of life. One must connect to the fullest extent possible, breathe the air in Hawai'i, share the breathe of the Hawaiian elders before one can say the aloha spirit lives in me".

Your lomi experience will be unique to you! Your lomi experience will change as you change and shift. Your experience will not compare to someone else's. The best lomi experiences are the ones that have no words to describe.

E hō mai
by Edith Kanaka'ole

(repeated 3 times)

E hō mai ka 'ike mai luna mai e
O nā mea huna no'eau o na mele e
E hō mai, e hō mai, e hō mai e

Grant us knowledge from above
The things of knowledge hidden in the chants
Grant us these things

CHAPTER FOUR

~ *Healing* ~

"Each persons' life is like a mandala, a vast limitless circle. We stand in the center of our own circle and everything we see, hear and think forms the mandala of our life. There's not a drop of rain or a pile of dog poop that appears in your life that isn't the manifestation of enlightened energy, that isn't a doorway to (a)sacred world. It's up to you whether your life is a mandala of neurosis or a mandala of sanity."

~ Pema Chodron

Healing takes place on many levels. It may happen in ways we never expected. We may not even recognize it has happened until we notice a shift in our life. Perhaps our modern culture is so far removed from the knowing of our higher power, trusting our intuition, following our dreams and opening to spirit, that we forgot all that can aid in our healing process.

When I reflect upon my life, I know I am blessed. I have seen healing take place in many forms, like the simple smile that warms a heart. The intense use of breathwork that can shift the cellular memory for profound release; a gentle hug that can bring tears to your eyes when you haven't been touched for ages. The healing touch of a massage therapist that soothes your nerves, restores your spirit and rejuvenates your body. Right down to the chicken soup your momma gave you when you were sick.

How does one heal?

I can only speak from my personal experiences and my heart on this topic.

"Face the simple fact before it becomes involved.
Solve the small problem before it becomes big."

~ Lao-Tzu

THE HEALING PROCESS BEGINS

*The shell
must break,
before the
bird
can fly.*

~ Tennyson

Let me start by telling you a story of a journey I took to Egypt in 1999 so you can understand more fully the circle of life and how it brought me to know and heal through the love of lomilomi. Going to Egypt was a lifelong dream. I was destined to go one month after the death of my spouse. I believe this was divinely planned. I had the opportunity to experience ancient beliefs and traditions as I walked through temples built in a time long past. It was a different way of looking at life. Looking upon the pillars carved of stone; the magnificent architecture and hieroglyphics, gave you a sense of the power, the struggles, the spiritual values and the mystery behind it all.

Travelling through the countryside, I witnessed the humble, simple life of the peasants and farmers. Small children stood by the wayside smiling and waving, appearing perfectly content, as our bus passed by. Plush fields of alfalfa grew for miles and the native Royal Palm, fig and date flourished everywhere, rendering an artist's delight. Observing this beauty, simplicity and all the happy smiles confirmed that there is beauty in everything and that we can achieve a state of happiness no matter where or how we live.

Happiness, which was not in the realm of my thought at the moment, was everywhere. Why couldn't I grasp hold of that simplicity and see the beauty again? Why couldn't I understand that all of life has its purpose and reasons for our existence? The grief I had in my heart needed to heal.

As the journey continued through Luxor, we visited the Valley of the Kings. I remember slowly climbing the path with the sacred tour group thinking "why am I doing this?" Later we had time to explore on our own and we were told to stay in certain regions. I just sat and waited, until I heard a voice instruct me to walk up another pathway and take the fork in the road. As I looked around, no one was paying attention to me. I trusted my intuition and went to a region that was closed. I came upon a tomb that was locked and no one was in sight. I sat down by myself and looked down upon the Valley of the Kings, breathing deeply, feeling energized and taking in this magnificent view. For the moment, I was very

Machu Picchu

grateful to be there. I noticed a plaque nearby that referenced this tomb being the biggest and most magnificent, deepest tomb of the XVIIIth dynasty. Suddenly out of nowhere, came an Egyptian man. In broken English he tried to communicate saying, "I got key". I was a bit frightened and I thought, "I can't go in there alone with him". Then a force from somewhere pushed me to go and so I followed. He tried to explain to me in simple English about the various gods and goddesses that were magnificently carved and painted on the walls. We walked what seemed like miles when he came to a stop. He pointed down into a chamber. There was a ladder. He motioned that I should come along. Hesitantly, I began to climb down the ladder, when a sense of peace and calm came over me. No fear even though I was alone with this strange man deep within a tomb where the sarcophagus of the king resided. Standing in awe I witnessed a granite structure colorfully decorated and beautifully carved. In this moment I knew why I was here.

Later, I asked the man if I could be alone for a moment and oddly enough he seemed to understand. I meditated and new I was ready for an initiation of some sort. I knew it was time to let go of something or someone and bring closure to a part of my life (*ho'oponopono*). But was I ready? I had been guided here by spirit to release the wedding band of my recently deceased husband. I felt I was not ready. I took a deep breath, sighed and tears rolled down my face. My heart was vibrating and my body was trembling. I felt the presence of something greater than I, something I had never experienced before of this magnitude.

We walked slowly out of the tomb. The man closed the gate and suddenly disappeared as quickly as he had arrived. I sat and I listened. I recalled the magical day of our wedding ceremony on the beach. The angelic Celtic harpist played "First Time Ever I Saw your Face", the song my spouse chose to dedicate to me. The exchange of love and the feeling inside me now was overwhelming. I knew I was not alone. There was a gentle presence

"A broken heart is an open heart"

~ *Elizabeth Lesser*
author of
Broken Open

Great Pyramid, Egypt

around me, a warmth on my shoulder, a soft breeze kissing my face. Then with a gentle but firm touch on my shoulder I heard in a loud voice as if God spoke from the heavens, "It is time to move on". My heart pounded, yet I felt a sense of overwhelming peace flood through me. I quickly buried his wedding band and ran down the pathway, where the group was already boarding the bus. I was breathing deeply and I was feeling exhilarated.

Healing was happening in this moment and I had no idea where it would lead next. "Could it happen this quickly?" I thought. I surrendered to the possibility. There is limitless possibility of bliss when we allow healing. I could not turn back.

I thought, was this trip to Egypt so divinely aligned, when I booked it three years previously, that spirit knew this would be the place I would so quickly begin my healing and learn about the spirit world? Was I sent here to connect and open a channel to my ancestors ('Aumakua)?

The simple answer is YES.

DIVINE GUIDANCE IN ACTION

It was on this trip in Egypt that my connection for Hawaii was made. I met a woman on this tour who would be the catalyst for me to pursue a trip to Hawaii later that year.

Several weeks later, when I was home I received a phone call from this woman. She remembered me and that I was a teacher in the healing arts. Her plan was to create a healing retreat and she invited me to speak. Hesitantly, I did not feel I would be ready and I questioned my ability to teach about healing anymore. Encouraging me to plan for it 8 months out, I said I would see what I could do.

Looking back at this, although her retreat never happened, she was the divine catalyst for me to arrive on the islands of Hawaii where my life was going to shift again. To find Lomilomi.

Had I not paid attention or followed through on any of these 'leads' where would I be today? Definitely not telling you this story and sharing the healing of lomilomi.

HEALING THE HEART

While in Cairo I had a dream. Simply, I was told to go to Peru and do missionary work. I never wanted to go to Peru. I questioned in my journal, was I sent to Egypt to get a message to go to Peru, Why? I ignored it for two years.

In those two years, coincidences where

happening all around me. HA! No coincidence I say. I even met a Peruvian shaman when I was teaching a class on cranial sacral therapy. Imagine that!

Then one day I received an email from an unknown individual. The information was about a journey to Peru. I truthfully did not read the details and just took it as another sign and responded, please send me information. Within a week I had a manila envelope in my hand from Mama Sharon. I began to shake and tremble as the energy flowed through me, yes, once again! With my hands trembling, barely able to open the envelope, I pulled out the paperwork and the business card fell on the floor. I picked it up and called Dr. Sharon Forrest and blindly said 'sign me up'. I had no idea what I was signing up for at this time. Weeks before my trip I read the itinerary. It was then I realized I would be going on a missionary trip. On the plane I thought, "Ok, I will go and do this but I have no idea why".

It didn't take long in Peru for me to realize I was being shown yet again another humble (ha'aha'a) lifestyle of homeless children who lived in joy. So open hearted they would greet us and laugh with us as we gifted them 1 crayon or 1 piece of paper. I was humbled (ha'aha'a) by their courage (koa) and spirit!

The final trek was to an orphanage high in the Andes. It was a long and bumpy ride. There were over 700 children in this remote place with no bathrooms, beds or enough food to feed all of them sufficiently. As sad as it seemed to me, coming from a country where we take for granted , in my opinion, that there is enough food daily, that we have a warm home and comfortable clothes and there isn't much to want for in most moments; I was in awe of the joy that emanated from this group of children. A group of 4 to 5 year olds wrapped their arms around me as I began to play ring around the rosey with them. We did not speak the same language with words, but we spoke the same from the heart (pu'uwai).

Ahhh, I knew in this moment our creator wanted my heart opened now. I smiled and laughed and felt the joy of these beautiful children. There was a smile on my face once

"The peoples of ancient Egypt, Greece, China and Japan practiced massage.

The voyagers from the South Pacific who first discovered Hawai'i more than 1200 years ago brought massage with them, just as they brought food staples, farm animals and medicinal herbs.

Once they settled the land, their massage techniques changed and evolved to become uniquely hawaiian.

As an indigenous practice, lomilomi varied, by ahupua'a (districts) and by 'ohana (family)."

~ Makana Rissa Chai,
Hawaiian Massage *
Lomilomi
Sacred Touch of Aloha

again; there was an energy in my being, in my soul, that was seemingly lost for a few years.

One young boy about 9 years old came up to me. He handed me the piece of paper we had given him moments before. One of our guides translated what he had written. He was giving thanks to the angels that came from God to share their heart with the children. I cried and cried because it was not *I* who shared my heart. It was *they* who opened my heart. The blessings bestowed upon me in this moment opened my heart center larger than I had ever dreamed imaginable. I realized truthfully, how selfish I was, how closed I was and how unappreciative I

truly was with my life. I was so self absorbed. I wanted to die… until now.

HEALING THE EMOTIONS

Returning from Peru I found out my business was going under. I took another deep breath and got on the plane from Kaua'i to New Jersey where my school was located, unannounced. I did not want to be angry. So I prayed for peace and understanding and the ability to forgive (*ho'oponopono*).

It turned out the accountant was embezzling from me and the new administrator forged my name by order of the accountant who didn't want to bother me. I felt numb in a way, but realized soon that I had become so unattached to the mundane trivial anomalies of life. I was playing witness and observing the people around me, their reactions, their excuses and yet I was not being affected by the deceit nor the emotions that might have once overtaken me. My heart was in a place that knew forgiveness and understood the elemental forces had a greater plan. I closed up shop, walked away and thought I would never teach again. Need I laugh? I am continually reminded that when spirit has a greater plan for our soul's purpose, you will soon become an observer of your life and learn to forgive more easily and let it go!

HEALING THE SPIRIT

When I took my next walk along the white sandy beaches of Kaua'i, I could've been angry. I realized I had no income and had to start life completely over. I picked up my pace and called out to *ke Akua* and suddenly I felt the release of a burden that had been on my shoulders for 12 years. It was gone. Gone was the stress of coming up with a monthly budget to support the school. Gone was the responsibility of administrating every aspect of a business. Gone were the headaches and long hours I placed upon myself that rolled into another day and more. I thought, you (*ke Akua*) freed up my life in order for me to live once again. I laughed. Why? Because I had made a vow at my wedding ceremony that I would free up my life and have time. Time for living and the universe heard me. Remember, that saying "Be careful what you ask for"?

Yes, healing can happen anywhere, anytime, any place if you just allow yourself to receive. Often we are looking for more profound answers, miracles to happen, that we miss the subtle messages and the path to healing that lies right before us.

Lomilomi is about the heart and opening to spirit. It is about healing on all levels. Once we can accept that healing is something that happens beyond the physical and includes the mind and spirit, we can begin to understand the profound effects of our thoughts and prayers, laughter, community and herbal medicines. Everything plays a huge role for what is needed in these times of transition!

Healing comes through with every *pule*.

Healing comes through counsel and *Hoʻoponopono*.

Healing comes through *Haʻa Haʻa*, Humility.

Healing comes through shifting energy, *Lomilomi*.

Healing happens through the divine elemental forces of nature.

Healing happens when you open to receive, *Aloha*!

So I am spirit and I am here to teach you the same! This is the healing path called A L O H A.

HEALING THE BODY

It is taught in lomilomi, the touch to the body may be the last thing we provide to assist with healing. The body consists of all levels and the physical manifestation is the lowest or last that may need the healing. Once we experience physical pain, we have missed the signs before us. When I thought it was time to leave the islands I experienced back pain that would stop me in my tracks. However, did I listen? No! Was

Love is natural

When we do not act out of love it goes against our very nature.

That choice results in emotional, mental and even physical pain.

Love heals the pain that was caused by the absence of it. Always act out of love.

~ Doe Zantamata

"We have something to work on, something to work with! God put us on this earth-plane completely equipped to have a happy and fulfilled life".

~ Change We Must, Nana Veary ~

I playing with fate yet again and "thinking" I knew what was next on my path? Perhaps. Was it coincidence that my back went into extreme spasm after receiving a chiropractic adjustment, only to find out much later, it was actually herniated? Was I to learn at some point that the energy that was weakening my system was going to teach me about the foundation of my life? Absolutely!

My life rapidly changed and the vital person I was began to deteriorate. I was living, or should I say existing now, in a region that did not support me well. I was in a relationship that was changing and yet I chose to believe it was the situation of our circumstances and did not recognize the energetic shifts that were speaking loud and clear to me. I found myself stressed, challenged and confused. Of course relationships go through this and why should I think for one moment it was not a test to survive and work through these challenging times. So I did. The pain became more intense and more chronic. There were many days I could not lift my body from the bed without assistance and always with excruciating pain. I forced myself to do daily chores, go to work, be a good partner and make the best of one of the most challenging and discouraging parts of my life. The pain got worse by the week. I am not one that takes any medication and I don't particularly like to utilize medical doctors. I tried what I knew holistically to make this pain go away. My days consisted of living in a physical environment that was not conducive to what I knew my spirit and self enjoyed. It began to drain my energy. I was working in a place that less than filled my spirit but had to help pay the bills. I was missing the islands immensely. I was not happy or feeling fulfilled. I questioned how I got here because I thought I was surrendering to the plan. Ahhh, it was in *the* plan but I didn't know it at the time. It was to teach me, again, how easily we can receive lessons, perhaps through a soul contract, to learn about discernment.

The journey continued and over the course of 3 years the pain grew worse and the limitations were plentiful. It seemed everything in my life was becoming more challenging as well. I questioned myself "Was I just being resistant to change...

Was I angry because of the changes... was I creating this pain in some way?" I am sure on some level a "yes" response to all those questions would apply. However, the deeper meaning and lessons were to come soon.

Finally, I went to see an orthopedic surgeon. He uttered the following words to me "If you don't get surgery, you will never walk again". Immediately, a surge of energy went through my spine and I replied to the doctor "Wipe that thought from your head". I realized in that moment that my frustration and anger was a motivator to heal my body. I took responsibility on every level to witness, to act upon and to utilize the knowledge available to heal my body. I decided, in that moment, I would take back *my power* and LET IT GO.

I remembered how I felt in Hawaii. How nature was my healer and the use of the breath was powerful. I felt connected. Bingo! I was not connected to Source. I began to spend more time in nature, move more, breathe more and listen more. I found new ways to move in my body that would soon teach me there are limitless possibilities if we open to them. I refused to give up and I was going to heal my body.

One day I realized how I lost touch with my soul's mission. I had given away my energy, my time and my love to other projects that were not my own. I thought I was being a good partner by doing this and working as a family unit. What I found out in truth was I gave away my soul. I was helping, something I knew how to do well, but I was not helping myself. I was out of balance. In that moment, I proclaimed I would get back on my path! The back began to heal, the pain subsided and I was feeling the connection to the spirit of *Aloha* once again. I fully immersed myself in teaching again. I found myself back on the island of Kaua'i experiencing what I thought I had lost.

I came home excited. The feeling stayed with me. I was to find out in the near future the relationship would not continue. I became truthful with myself, once more. I looked deep inside and realized that when your soul is not supported on its mission and those in your life do not support its growth, life will change. It is up to us how we choose to allow these changes to affect us. Life shifted again. While my heart was healing, my spirit was soaring.

"As we realize that God's mind is the basis of our individual consciousness, we begin to solve our problems at their point of origin, which is within ourselves. We need to repair the broken communication within ourselves. We must be honest with ourselves, forgive ourselves, get back in touch with the source, and all will be well."

~ Nana Veary

*"We are all
just walking
each other
home"*

~ Ram Dass

Magical connections were happening! Manifesting dreams were happening and the 'hook up' to *ke Akua* I thought I had lost, was just a breath away.

Another journey was about to begin. Healing is always happening if we pay attention. I remembered how to create *lokahi*. I remembered to live Lomilomi. I was being directed to teach lomilomi.

It is only when we stay stuck in that which does not serve us, that we disconnect from our truth. I ask you now, what prevents you from healing?

BOWL OF LIGHT
*We are each born with a
bowl of light
Full of ke Akua's love*

HULI THE BOWL
*The stones symbolize the negativity
We can bring into our life
Each night we turn it over to
Begin a new day with a Bowl of Light.*

CHAPTER FIVE

~ *Pule* ~

~ *It is not in the asking.*
It is in the grace and beauty of who you are ~

~ Ku'uleialoha from the Aloha Messages Cards

Pule or prayer is probably the single most important element of lomilomi. Every practitioner is taught to begin and end their session with *pule*. There is a reverence and respect for the connection with *ke Akua* (Creator). It is never underestimated that the healing a person may need will come through the *pule* at the level they have with their soul's contract. A *pule* can be chanted as in an *oli*, if the practitioner has studied such with a *kumu*. It is with the *oli* that the powerful *mana* shifts vibration and transcends the space of time in the present moment.

The Hawaiian language contains many vowels which resonate to our body. In Ayurvedic studies you learn how vowel sounds resonate to each chakra (wheel of energy). I have found that the Hawaiian chants are similar. They open blockages, connect on higher levels and provide a solid grounding force for healing to be facilitated.

In the late 90's while I lived on Kaua'i I was privileged to be a part of an ancient Hawaiian ceremony with a local family. We went to a hula *heiau* (sacred site or temple). There was a powerful yet gentle man who was known as a chanter. Upon entering this sacred site, an entry chant that vibrated from the depths of Pele gave us permission to enter. As I proceeded through the gateway with the *kumu*, I could actually feel a molecular change occurring within my entire being. I felt a portal (gateway) opening taking me back to a more ancient time and

Lei making is also a part of lomilomi

saw my body differently, as a young *wahine* (woman). The veil had been lifted. I was overwhelmed emotionally and an intense electrical energy ran through my body. My perception began to shift as I could see things from another time and place. In awe, I witnessed the group of students gracefully enter the *heiau*. Each person I looked at shifted and was no longer the person I knew just moments prior. There is no doubt from my vast experiences at many sacred sites on our planet with other shamans, that the power of vibration in chants can access another dimension or levels of awareness.

We prayed together with kumu. We gifted our leis at the altar of the spirit of the Goddess. It was my prayer that provided me with the grace to know who I am in that moment.

E ke Akua
Dearest Lord

Mahalo no
We thank thee

Mahalo ia oe
We especially thank thee

No kea ai
For this food

Amene

~ *Prayers to use for healing sessions* ~

LOMI PULE

E Aloha Mai
(Let there be love)

E Mana Mai
(Let there be spiritual power)

E Pono Mai
(Let there be truth)

E Ola no
(Let there be healing)

Amama ua noa
(So be it, it is done)

Mahalo ke Akua
for blessings great and small

Makaho ke Akua
our great love touches all

Let us be mirrors of your light

Keepers of your love

Mahalo ke Akua
for your blessings from above

Aloha ke Akua

We ask for your protection
and blessings

From the top of our head
to the soles of our feet

To the four corners of our body

Wherever it is needed to go

Mahalo

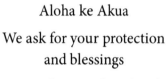

In the name of_____
and through our prayers

I lift off whatever there is of heaviness
and with love send it to the light

I stand at the source
with the Divine Creator

Who walks with me
through all changes in life

I am here with you

CHAPTER SIX

~ Hā - The Breath~

Hā means life and to exhale. Hawaiians understood the connection of breathing with their life force.

They might forcefully breathe the Hā to an affected region of the body for healing.

Ku'uleialoha breathes 'ola into her hands and oil before applying it to her client.

The *Hā* is the breath and essence of *ke Akua* (God/Creator). Through a variety of breathing techniques we may learn many things including how to relieve stress, clear our minds, eliminate pain and build our *mana* (spiritual energy). The breath has been used in many cultures and is very popular in yogic practices as the key to healing. The *Hā Breath* is a key component not only for the practitioner, but for the client as well. The *hā* brings *ola*, life force energy, to both. It also assists in moving energy through the practitioner, for clearing. The breath can easily be utilized to clear out headaches, help one focus and calm the mind. A lomi practitioner will build their *mana* with the *hā* while they also perform martial arts as preparation for a session. Thirty *hā* breaths done daily for a month can shift your vibration and bring more peace and calm in your life. Inhale and exhale for twice as long. Ex. inhale to a count of 4 , exhale to a count of 8.

The Hawaiians have a term *haole* meaning one without breath or the spirit of *ke Akua*. When the missionaries came to the islands the word *haole* was thought to mean white man when it was really an expression of individuals who did not hold the spirit of the creator within.

I can personally attest to the power of healing with the breath. I used the *hā* in two situations which included my herniated disc and a fractured rib. Both were extremely painful. In my infinite stubbornness to listen to the medical doctor who said it would take 6 weeks to heal the rib, I began to utilize the *hā* breath for 2 weeks and my rib was healed.

Breathe with conscious intention. Keep your thoughts clear while breathing. Lack of proper breathing can be the cause of many tension based illnesses. Sit up straight, focus and align yourself with the universe. Now breathe out the tension and breathe in new life.

CHAPTER SEVEN

~ 'Ohana ~

~ Breathing in and out,
True listening reflects who we are in relationship
Deepen your connection to the sacred family ~

~ Ku'uleialoha from the Aloha Messages Cards

The concept of *'ohana*, family and extended family or community, is the basis of all Hawaiian values. It extends beyond to all that exists in the universe. This has been a powerful concept to bring to my students. By creating a cohesive living environment in our intensive trainings, we share responsibilities to cooperate, honor and respect each other along with sharing daily chores. The Hawaiians knew this was the natural way. They had a personal relationship with everything: the *'Aumakua* (ancestors), the *āina* (nature) and the *'ohana* (community). They had reverence for mother earth and taught the *keiki* (children) how to honor and respect the *āina* for generations, similar to other indigenous teachings.

The *'ohana* taught the children the lineage, the language, how to fish and build canoes. Each *'ohana* had different gifts and skills that their lineage depended upon. The *kupuna* (elders) taught them also about *ha'a ha'a* (humility). Many of these values have been lost in the traditional modern culture. However, the sense of this tribal loss is creating the need for connections again. People are seeking wisdom and reaching out for their *'ohana* to connect once again with their culture.

Support is the essential foundation and essence that encourages growth of the spirit through a loving process. Through this support we grow as individuals more fully and wholly. In allowing our *'ohana* to share, we honor their gifts and value their

Caroline Myss speaks about us looking for our tribe. Finding our connections through our root chakra, our foundation.

Author of

Anatomy

of the Spirit

> *"Conversation
> is the vehicle for
> setting boundaries
> and allowing our
> authentic heart to
> be seen. It conveys
> the landscape of
> your inner life,
> your feelings, wants
> and musings. The
> commitment to
> open, honest kind
> communication
> forges a foundation
> that nurtures love;
> it builds a bridge of
> intimacy between
> two worlds. Conflicts
> can be resolved and
> closeness deepened
> by contacting and
> speaking from your
> authentic heart."*
>
> *~ John Amodeo, PhD*

spirit's mission. To receive support opens the *pu'uwai* to wholeness.

I have learned several lessons in my life about reaching out for this support and how crucial it is in one's life. It makes everyone feel helpful and worthwhile and supported.

LISTENING

In November of 2012, *ke Akua* sent me on a mission. I didn't know exactly what it was going to be, however, for months I knew something was up. I was teaching on the Hawaiian islands when one morning I "knew" I must shorten my trip and get home. I still did not know why. I shared this feeling with Kumu Karen Leialoha. She said "well you know you must listen". 30 minutes later, we returned to our vehicle and it had been broken into . In a moment I utilized my *hā* breath and relaxed into forgiveness. I asked Kumu to perform *ho'oponopono* (to make things right through forgiveness) around the car with the students. The students said to me later "You really walk your talk". I stayed calm and realized everything had a purpose.

Four days passed before I could return home. Upon my arrival home, I placed my suitcases down when my phone rang. I heard from an Angel, a former student by that name. New Jersey had been hit with Hurricane Sandy. A mutual colleague of ours lost everything, including her massage table. Angel asked if it was possible to find her a table. Without hesitation, the *mana* was building, I could feel it powerfully running through me as I made some calls. The sense to help *'ohana* was immediate, no hesitation as the force within grew stronger to help. This energy can be compared to that of a torus, an energetic pattern that is in every living system. I was feeling this and it became a part of me. Soon I would feel the greatness of spirit and the co-creation of a larger *'ohana*. A non-profit formed "Massage Without Borders". Massage Therapists Helping Massage Therapists. This was the greater plan that *ke Akua* had in mind. The *mana* has not stopped. To be of service to our community is a gift that the soul fulfills when you listen to the calling. This is a living lomi. This is what my kumu taught me.

The balance between spirit, nature and mankind and the *mana* grew stronger and the connection to *ke Akua*. I was definitely "hooked up".

When we provide this safety net for our *'ohana*, the families will thrive, the planet will thrive and we can teach others how to bring this into their lives to create *lōkahi*.

It is because of this profound understanding and sense of community, that I have given my service to my *haumana* (students). I vowed to be there when they need me for encouragement, support, guidance and love. I have created over the years a supportive network that, until this non-profit, I had not realized how strong it was. This type of community service opens the heart to joy and Aloha and allows us to bring this wisdom around the world.

It was through my cultural studies and practice of lomilomi that I brought *'ohana* back into my life. Everything I have been sharing is part of this whole healing system, this lifestyle, lomilomi!

"The whole of planet Earth is a sacred site.

All people are the chosen people, and the purpose of our lives is a spiritual one.

May we care for each other, and the earth, for everything relates to everything else.

Feeling this oneness, may we radiate the light of love and kindness that all may live in unity and peace."

~ Radha Sahar

As social animals a key factor to our living a happy life is friendship, trust and openness. We are all the same as members of one human family. Trust is the basis of friendship and we'll find this if, in addition to the knowledge we gain from ordinary education, we develop warm-heartedness. This gives rise to self-confidence and inner strength, which through trust and friendship leads to co-operation with others. ~ Dalai Lama

CHAPTER EIGHT

~ *Mana* ~

Mana has been described to me as spiritual energy, a heightened level of spiritual awareness, a healing power, or an energy which empowers all living things or creatures. *Mana* was only an idea, a concept and a feeling I thought I knew and understood. It was during an experience at the Waipa Foundation on the island of Kaua'i, that I began to understand the true meaning of *mana*.

The Waipa Foundation serves as a Hawaiian community learning center. It is a place where you can reconnect with 'āina and renew your sense of 'ohana while working with your hands (*laulima*). The stewardship of the 1,600 acre *ahupua'a* is under the Waipa Foundation, a non-profit organization, the board, staff, participants and volunteers of which represent our community including the *kupuna. Kalo* or taro is the staple plant that Hawaiians process into *poi. The poi* is made by pounding (in ancient times) the taro root, after a steaming process and creating a pudding like consistency. Today more modern methods might include grinders to process the taro after it has been steamed, cleaned, sorted, cleaned again, prayed upon and loved. The Hawaiians believe your state of being and your words all go into the making of *poi.*

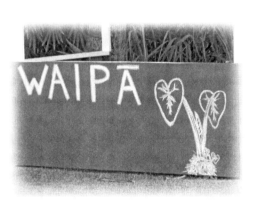

So in traditional style I will tell you another story to teach you and help you understand how *mana* is created.

Prior to teaching lomilomi on Kaua'i, I was in *pule* when I received the message to take my students to make *poi.* I did not question this and immediately contacted a Hawaiian friend on the islands to find out if there was a place our group could participate in this sacred process. We were lead to the Waipa Foundation. Upon contacting the Waipa Foundation, I was welcomed to bring my students, however, I was asked if we knew an entry chant (*oli*). My response was no, but that I would make sure we learned one to honor their tradition. I was then advised we needed to have the group there before sunrise at approximately 5 A.M. to be welcomed by the *kupuna*. I thought, "Oh my, that is early!" I agreed we would honor their tradition and planned to see them soon.

While on the island, Kumu Leilani Kaleiohi had only a few hours to teach our group an entry chant. In her joyful laughter at the *heiau* (sacred site), she assured us we could do this and honor her lineage. We didn't have quite the confidence she attempted to infuse into our souls, although we would give it our best shot.

If you ever tried to speak Hawaiian, you will know the pronunciations may bring challenges. Now try to chant with the intention and passion behind the words you barely know or can pronounce. I can assure you, you most definitely will push yourself through limitations and be persistent to succeed with respect and honor for your *kumu*.

The group had excitement, doubt, fear and anticipation as to whether or not they would be able to honorably chant for the *kupuna* and be welcomed onto the plantation. Diligently, two of my assistants practiced for hours in hopes they could lead the group early the next morning. The moment arrived and we arose at 3:30 a.m. to prepare for our journey to Waipa. In silence, we gracefully entered the vehicles in preparation to participate in a rare and sacred practice of love. As we drove along the north shore under the indigo skies, we practiced until we came to the region that opens to the portal of the taro fields. In silence we prayed as the journey continued. I pulled the van onto the grass parking lot and stepped outside under the brilliant sky to greet one of the *kupuna* preparing under the tent. I silently walked on these sacred lands, breathing, smelling the freshness of the day and noticing the abundance of stars twinkling above me, sending greetings from the '*Aumakua* (ancient ones).

The elder looked up to greet me, tears rolled down his aged face while he hugged me. He looked beyond to see a group of twenty others waiting anxiously to be accepted into their presence. He explained the protocol to me and asked me to wait with the group until the

other *kupuna* arrived. I was received with such *mana* and *aloha* that I instantly felt a shift in my being. I walked proudly back to my group, feeling like I was being embraced by the entire universe. We waited quietly.

I looked up about ten minutes later to see a group of *kupuna* standing like the royal guard under the tent. They chanted to us, the signal for our group to offer our entry chant. We stood in awe and full of pride. With our intention we did our best to present our offering to the *kupuna* in hopes that we would be accepted. Then there was silence. A long silence. A powerful voice chanted across the valley touching our hearts, followed by a profound silence. Finally, the words *Aloha* as the *kupuna* welcomed this group with open arms. Our hearts were pounding and yet there was a sense of something more powerful pulling us into the center of this community. In moments, we were sitting with the *kupuna*, peeling and cleaning the kalo, laughing and sharing stories

There were smiles worn on our faces and in our hearts. I saw and sensed an energy more intense spinning through this 'ohana very rapidly and easily. Joy emanated everywhere and in everyone. The kalo was receiving this beautiful mana, which would be the poi that would feed a community. Any previous sense of time, no longer existed. Not one person was concerned about being tired, for the energy was high. Not one person missed eating breakfast because they were being fed by the *mana*.

First stages of cleaning the taro

The students were guided into different positions as the progression of the poi making process unfolded. The *kupuna* were in complete and utter gratitude constantly saying *mahalo* (thank you).

I recall wearing a constant big smile on my face witnessing the love of 'ohana. It was this love that created more *mana*. It was this *mana* that was providing us abundant energy and joy. Time went slowly and quickly as if we were walking in two worlds. By 9 A.M. the process was completed and the *kupuna* expressed thankfulness, sharing with us that this process typically takes all day. Their gratitude for our support was immense and yet I can see we did not fully understand in this moment what was really happening.We sat with the *kupuna* still sharing stories and learning about the importance of knowing our lineage and speaking about *ke Akua's* love. The students began to gift the *kupuna* with lomi chair massage as they sat receiving the love openly. I saw on the faces of the students a joy of gratitude for this moment of sharing. I felt something was shifting within them, while beams of light were blessing their hearts. One of the *kupuna*, gently grabbed my hand while two of the students stood by her side. She said, "Keep teaching what you are teaching, for I have not felt spirit in me for a long time. *Mahalo*". We all had tears of joy flowing down our cheeks.

I looked around again and saw and felt the *mana* circulating everywhere. Laughter was in the air, love was in the heart and joy was building in every moment. Every person was sharing and caring. I suggested we perform our hula for the *kupuna*. We did not know all the steps yet, however, I was sure in my heart they would appreciate our efforts and feel our respect. One of my assistants who had lovingly shared her gifts all week, led our group. We sang White Sandy Beach. The students were excited to dance. The *kupuna* sat respectfully watching our *halāu* proudly move in grace and love. This moment built even more *mana* and no one was ashamed or conscious of our steps being performed correctly. It was perfectly and divinely offered as a gift. It was the intention. The smile on my face was pasted across my cheeks when I realized it had not stopped for the last six hours. I stepped back to observe the group once again, share more hugs, more *aloha*, more stories, and more *mana*.

A group of young students arrived. They stood honorably as they chanted for the *kupuna*. My students stood humbled when they realized the respect and diligence these young children demonstrated. Every child came up to greet us with a hug of aloha as this is the way. It is the *kuleana* (responsibility) of their *kumu* (teachers) to impress upon them they must respect their *kupuna* (elders). This was also something my parents taught me as a child.

It was only 11:30 a.m. and we began to prepare to find our way back to our *hale* (house). No one could believe it was so early. No one could believe they were so energized! The hugs began as we bid the Waipa Foundation volunteers and the *kupuna* aloha. We were gifted with *taro* and *poi* to take back to our *hale* and share with our ʻ*ohana*, infused with this beautiful *mana*. The vibrancy in each student was better than Christmas morning. Laughter and happy chattering voices filled my ears with a loving energy. I was so glad I listened to the message I heard only two weeks prior to take my students to make *poi*. This was quite an experience.

Making *poi* as ʻ*ohana* was the *mana*! Starting from the gift of the *āina*, the vibrant energy of the *taro*, the honorable preparation and *pule*. The joy of giving and sharing *aloha* with ʻ*ohana* among every participating member, all created the *mana*. It was the *lōkahi* we will speak about in Chapter 13. It was the pinnacle point above the triangle that connects us with spirit. It is *mana*!

ʻOhana making poi with Kealoha Saffery

CHAPTER NINE

~ *Pono* ~

"If it is good, if it is in balance, if it is right, if it helps, if it is righteous,
if it corrects, if it is responsible, if it is caring, if it is humble,
if it is peaceful, if it honors, it is pono."

~ Pali Jae Lee

"What is true?

Can you

absolutely know

it's true?"

~ Byron Katie
author of
Loving What Is

The principle of *Pono* has brought me to many questions.

Am I to understand truth to be universal as in a collective conscious or on a singular basis? Am I to understand your truth may be different than mine and we might agree to disagree harmoniously? Might there be a truth we have yet to discover that will open the hearts of each individual to set aside their differences? Might it include honoring ones truth in their moment? Will we be shown a divine truth beyond our human comprehension? My answer would be yes to all of the above.

Byron Katie's two simple questions can help us come to a greater understanding when questioning truth. What we see or feel is true in one moment can completely change when we ask our self is it absolutely true for another? How could we possibly know unless there was effective communication?

Our relationship with all beings will teach us these lessons. As we learn to communicate from our heart we will come to understand from this place. If we listen to our intention and cause no harm with our actions or deeds, we will be in balance.

In the Hawaiian culture they use a system called *ho'oponopono*, to set things right and bring balance to a situation. The entire family might come together to discuss a problem or situation at hand. During *ho'oponopono* they would all try their best to understand and listen in order to find a solution and resolve it satisfactorily.

If I have offended you, your family, and ancestors in thoughts, words, deeds or actions at any time, I am sorry.

Please forgive me. I love you.

If you have ever taken anger management classes or communication classes, you might find similarities with this process. When you learn and understand how to work diligently and bring balance to the situation at hand without being charged and angry then you can Let It Go ~ Then you are in *Pono*.

Wayne Kealohi Powell shares Kumu Harry's ideas in an essay about *ho'oponopono*: "Freedom from the soul achieved through a revelation of consciousness that sees everyone as innocent and equally loved, loving and lovable. To release all resentments and judgments requires that complete wholeness returns to the being, putting an end to separation and fragmentation." Wayne continues to reflect on Harry's teachings "In this place, this space, the reigning idea is that, as God sees us, no one is above another. So humans see God in every form, and in no form there is not God's presence."

"Walk and touch peace every moment.

Walk and touch happiness every moment.

Each step brings a fresh breeze.

Each step makes a flower bloom.

Kiss the Earth with your feet.

Bring the Earth your love and happiness.

The Earth will be safe

when we feel safe in ourselves."

~ Thich Nhat Hahn

CHAPTER TEN

~ 'Aumakua ~

"Hamoea is the principal goddess of those who practice the art of massage"

~ Joseph S. Emerson 1918

The *'aumakua* are our guides and ancestors. The Hawaiians might have spirit guides through the *pōhaku* (stones) or sea life, birds, etc. Deities were called *'aumakua* and they could be called upon for protection, comfort and spiritual support.

The *'Aumakua*, the ancestors who have crossed over the rainbow bridge, often had their bones specially stripped of flesh upon death. They would be wrapped in *kapa* and ceremonially prepared. The bones were placed in the custody of another descendant. Mary Kawena Pukui, a scholar of Hawaiian culture, who died in 1986 at age 91, explained: "As gods and relatives in one, they give us strength when we are weak, warning when danger threatens, guidance in our bewilderment, inspiration in our arts. They are equally our judges, hearing our words and watching our actions, reprimanding us for error and punishing us for blatant offense."

In lomilomi we call out to our *'Aumakua* to provide us with the wisdom and knowledge we will need to be of service. It is important for you to know your ancestry, their gifts and the lineage that has gone before them. There may be times when this information is not available and you may say your *pule* and feel it in your heart and soul. The *'aumakua* continue to be revered by many a Hawaiian family.

Lōkahi Message

~ Ku'uleialoha

Do not let the water drown you
Or the wind knock you down
Do not let the fire burn you

Allow the mother to support you and
Teach you through the winds of time

It is in the flow of the seas
And the passionate fire that lives within
Where Lōkahi lives

Let no one disturb that peace!

It must be that you come together from the same source, the āina
It must be that you share the same breath, Hā
It must be that balance exists within

There is a time where all meet ke Akua
In the moment of peace
When heaven and earth meet as the rays of light are shared
Then ke Akua's hand touches you and you know

You have received the gifts of Aloha
to learn the skills on your journey to harmony.

CHAPTER ELEVEN

~ *Acknowledging our Kumu* ~

Consciousness is happening on many levels
Let patience take it's time ~ Let it flow
Spiritual alignment will be divinely ordained
~ AHONUI ~

~ Ku'uleialoha from the Aloha Messages Cards

A *kumu* is a teacher. A *kahuna* is a keeper of the knowledge and wisdom who oversees the structure of the Hawaiian life and culture. They might be healers, advisors, astrologers and keepers of the family genealogy. They are the keeper of all sacred things. A *kumu* may also be a *kahuna*.

A *kahuna* honored the Hawaiian traditional system by keeping information secret. These secrets are only passed onto a few chosen ones. The chosen one would spend many years witnessing and learning by *experience*. There were no books to learn from and information was passed on through oral tradition and stories. The *kahuna* would expect you to learn about your life through your soul's mission. They might ask you "Why are you here?" You learned about your purpose. You played witness to nature and her cycles. You learned about the *kuleana* (responsibility) you have on your life path. The secrets would be made known to you when you paid attention diligently. Lomilomi would soon become a part of your life.

Aunt Margaret Machado

Aunty Margaret Machado *(1916-2009).* Aunty was born and raised on the Big Island of Hawai'i. She was known to be the first Hawaiian to receive her massage license. Sharing the loving touch of God with others was the primary mission in her life.

Never let the sun go down with an angry heart was her philosophy.

We give thanks to all her gifts and for sharing this healing system with so many people across the world. Aunty was the first to share lomilomi with non-hawaiians.

Kahu Abraham Kawai'i

Kahu Abraham Kawai'i during a lomilomi

Kahu Abraham Kawai'i grew up in a small fishing village on the Big Island. He began to teach Ka Huna bodywork in the late 1960's. "It was his desire", shares his surviving partner Ho'okahai Tamara, to grace us with this art. He taught us how to provide a space to heal and grow to our fullest potential".

Kahu taught "There is always a Yes". It would be through moving past your obstacles that you would then be able to teach others. He taught about aligning yourself with the nature and cycles of life. This would teach us how to flow in our own life.

Aunty Angeline Locey

Kumu Michael Locey

Aunty Angeline Locey lives on the island of Kaua'i. Aunty began her path in lomi when she was in her 50's where she had a homecoming to her own culture, transforming her life. She has a joyful, beautiful spirit. In 1985, she opened her institute Mu'olaulani Hawaiian Wellness Center in Anahola. Aunty described lomilomi to me as "open heart surgery" in her innocent and sweet manner.

Kumu Michael Locey, originally from Oahu, now lives on the island of Kaua'i. He is the caretaker of his mother's Wellness center and practices lomilomi with his wife and daughter. Michael feels it was a natural evolution to practice traditional Hawaiian healing treatments. He is also very conscious of our āina and creating eco-sustainability on our planet. Michael shares that lomilomi can be a self-actualization tool, focusing on the whole person. The chants that are used, call in ke Akua, speaking to the heart of lomilomi. They are the tools that go to the receiver of the lomi and the environment, depending on the intention.

I love bringing my students here to sit in the steam and receive a Hawaiian sea salt scrub.

www.angelineslomikauai.com

Kumu Brenda Mohalapua Ignacio, a native of the Big Island she later moved to Oahu. In 1975 she was a student of Nana Veary. It is her belief that in the sharing of the history and philosophy of this loving work, as well as performing this sacred touch with grace and a genuinely caring heart, others can awaken to and appreciate their own awareness of the healing power within. She shared with me that lomilomi is the embodiment of reverence for life, wisdom, knowledge and compassion. Kumu also teaches the practice of Ho'oponopono and shares her love of hula too!

Kumu Brenda gifted me with my Hawaiian name My child of God's Love.

Kumu Brenda
Mohalapua Ignacio

www.lomilomialoha.com

Kumu Harry Uhane Jim, born and raised on the island of Kaua'i, he now resides on the Big Island with his wife Sila. Lomilomi was handed down through his family and kupuna from the age of 5. Harry is the author of *Wise Secrets of Aloha*. Harry believes the human experience can create negative energy and turn it into positive forms once we embrace the paradox and change the chaotic patterns. He explains in his teachings, that the vibration one must manifest, distinctly defines the current of sacred space for lomilomi. Together with is wife Sila, they joyfully share their dynamic partnership through Aloha. Sila's grandfather was Papa Bray, a modern day kahuna.

Kumu Harry Uhane Jim

"Stop negotiating and start navigating!"

www.harryjimlomilomi.com

Kumu Karen Leialoha Carroll
Photograph by: Hokulii Images

Kumu Karen Leialoha Carroll

Kumu was born and raised on Oahu, and graduated from the Kamehameha Schools, an elite school for children of Hawaiian ancestry. She received a nursing degree and also interned with Papa Kalua Kaiahua, the great Hawaiian healer from Maui. She is descended from a family of spiritual healers from the Big Island and Oahu.

Kumu Karen can fill a room with joy and laughter instantly as she embodies the spirit of a child. She teaches about the importance of the unihipili (inner child) through her Hawaiian value lessons.

I credit Kumu Karen for teaching me the true essence and spirit of Alo~Ha. I cannot express enough gratitude for the wisdom she has passed onto me. When I asked her one evening "Why me?" she said, "Because it is your turn." The hearts connect, the love flows, the gifts are passed on as we honor and respect the ministry we serve through lomilomi.

www.kapuaokalani.com

Kumu Dane Kaohelani Silva grew up and lives on the Big Island of Hawai'i. He graduated from the University of Hawai'i with a degree in Biology and Liberal Studies (Biomedical Science). He received his doctorate in chiropractic with honors from Life Chiropractic College West. He learned lomilomi from his father, grandmother and kupuna from his family.

I give thanks to Kumu Dane for teaching me the importance of Lokahi during my visit to the Big Island. He told me it is the most important thing I can teach my students. As we sat in nature's school, he explains about the symbol of the triangle. He will discuss more on this in the Lokahi chapter. If there is no connection or 'ola (life force energy), we cannot build our mana. Our bodies represent the triangle as well. The feet can be compared to the base or the āina and 'ohana and our head or crown is compared to spirit or ke Akua.

http://haleola.com

Kumu Dane Silva

photographer: Kaori Mahelona

Penny Prior

Kumu Penny Prior lives on the island of Kaua'i and has been involved in the healing arts for over 30 years. She was introduced to lomilomi by Kahu Abraham Kawai'i in 1987 and was inspired to move to the islands. In 1992 Penny met hula master Kumu Hula Roselle Keli'ihonipua Bailey and joined her hula halāu. She loves to sing and play the ukulele.

www.hawaiianmassage.com

Kumu Ku'uipo Latonio grew up in Hawaii. Her family shared their love for aloha, food, hula and laughter. Ku'uipo co-created a lomilomi training with Penny Prior and taught together for 15 years.

Penny and Ku'uipo gave me my first exposure to lomilomi on Kaua'i in 1999. They provided an experience that changed the course of my life.

Ku'uipo Latonio

Nana Veary, author of *Change We Must* is a renowned Hawaiian born in 1908. I did not have the pleasure of personally meeting Nana, however she has been a huge influence in my heart and life. She taught about healing through all aspects of life and how everything is rooted in the cycles of nature. Her spiritual journey speaks of her truth and encourages us to find our own. Her story is powerful along with her beliefs. Her personal transformation is expressed through Aloha. Nana was known for giving you that extra kick you needed to move through your obstacles.

When I read Nana's book, I get inspired each time. I feel her presence and support. It is because of her life journey I am inspired to share mine.

As the years have gone by and many of the Kahuna have passed on we have lost much of the traditional ways. One of the last Hawaiian Kahuna, Makua shared much of his wisdom with his friend and author Hank Wesselman. *Bowl of Light* delves into a deeper understanding of the spiritual path through the eyes and lessons of Makua. I highly recommend reading this book.

I have learned through my diligent studies, that the reverence that is passed on through the Hawaiian lineage from the kupuna is not something you learn from a technique based massage course. This is something you experience and receive from the heart and breath of the elders with their blessings. I know these lessons will continue in my lifetime as I seek Lokahi.

I invite each of you to explore your growth potential and embrace the opportunity to be of service to mankind.

Mahalo nui loa to all the kumu who have touched my heart and my life.

CHAPTER TWELVE

Lomi
The Spirit of Aloha
Ku'uipo Latonio

Lomilomi means to rub, press or massage and break apart; and to me it also means, 'to put back together again with *aloha* - love, compassion and respect'. The form that I have been initiated into, teach and have great respect for is a nature based form of transformational bodywork which involves what is called 'Flight' movement, *hā* (breath), *pule* (prayer) and lots of *aloha*.

Penny Prior and I teamed up after I trained and apprenticed with her. We co-created and taught our lomi, nature based trainings together for 15 years. Out of these experiences we eventually entitled our trainings "Lomi Mai Ka Na'au", 'Lomi from the heart or center of the being'. The original version of this form came from Ka huna bodywork and Kahu Abraham Kawai'i.

It is a wonderful adventure in exploring the human body/being in a fluid and sensory dance using a form of navigation that is associated with nature and the elements…like a stream of water moving over, through and around the land. It invokes the divine feminine essence; a receptive, compassionate and deep flowing nature in both the giver and receiver.

Lomi is a way to cleanse congestion and old patterning from body, mind, emotions and spirit. It is also a rite that connects us with the ancestors, ascended masters, our higher selves as well as the *āina* to assist the individual with opening their hearts as well as to a conscious releasing of the past and accelerated growth into the future.

Lomi to us, as teachers and practitioners of this work, is a sacred way of life. We lomi not only the physical body during a session but also the 'being and spirit' of the person we are working with while at the same time we are using *pule* (prayer). We also lomi the *āina* (land), nature and the elements around us, our *'ohana*, our connections and relationships, our food, our songs, dances and practically every thing and situation in our lives. We lomi until we find ways to bring 'all' into *lōkahi* (balance) and harmony. This is all done with "the spirit of aloha".

To me the spirit of aloha is an attitude and a state of being that is about sharing and lightheartedness. It is about being present, open, warm, compassionate and receptive to ourselves and to others. It is also about being generous, connected, joyful, helpful and *pono* (true and respectable). To me, it is an inheritance and a certain gift that people of Hawaii demonstrate with one another, to our *'ohana* (family) – extended and visitors as well. It is a place where innocence lives, where we are free to share, forgive and express our hearts, our feelings through our being and our *kino* (body), our eyes, smiles, laughter, tears, music, *mele* (songs), hula and *lomi* (loving touch).

Also a part of the 'spirit of aloha' to me is the love of and sharing what provisions we have in the way of *kau kau* (food) (ono-lishess), fresh tropical fruit *'mo sweetah'* and the *la'au* (trees & plants), the *pua* (flowers) *'nani and onaona'* (beautiful and fragrant)…besides that the *mea ola* (living creatures of the *āina* (land)) and the beautiful *kai* (ocean) which are the real magic of the islands. As island people we are emerged in and learn from our environment early in and throughout life, *aloha āina* (love of the land) and appreciation of the elements, movement, sensuality and the beauty that nature constantly demonstrates. Each brings wonder, joy, wholeness and *nui na'auao* (much wisdom) to those who participate in these experiences. When the islands, the *nohona* (way of life) and the people come together in 'the spirit of aloha', all is *pono* (right), unified and harmonious! When *aloha* (love) is present anything is possible.

Growing up in Hawaii, many of my family members were very generous, sharing with one another whatever we had in ways we were able to. Visiting family was always a treat as not only were our visits filled with laughter, play, music, singing, dancing and exploring nature; we received plenty *ono* food placed out for everyone's enjoyment (my family were and are great cooks) and from the fresh abundance of the *āina*. Everyone always left feeling very happy and content.

When I was very young, one of my uncles used to go to the airport and greet strangers. He was very warm, happy and friendly so visitors would warm up to him right away. He would ask them if they had a place to stay and if they did not he would take them on a tour of some parts of the island and help them find a place to stay in the areas he thought were especially good. He would recommend places for them to eat and often take them home to my Aunty who would serve them whatever she made for dinner that night. There was always extra to share. Sometimes they would even invite certain folks to stay overnight until they found somewhere else to stay. This to me is the spirit of aloha which can still be discovered in many little pockets of *Hawaii nei*.

I loved our frequent family gatherings in Ala Moana Beach Park. There was an abundance of food, music, singing, camaraderie, laughter, lots of 'talk story' and dancing whether on land or in the water! It was always a lot fun and a true sharing of the aloha spirit amongst my family and it still is when we get together for family events and most recently my Auntie's 100th birthday celebration and family reunion this past year. This is aloha for me and I take it with me where ever I go.

Learning and teaching this form of lomi has been a huge blessing in my life, both on a personal and professional level. I am very grateful to Penny and all my teachers for sharing their aloha, *na'auao*, wisdom & knowledge, guidance, care, alliance and trust in my ability to carry on this lineage. I have great respect for them and all teachers of the sacred and healing arts that come from these islands and beyond.

Growing up in Hawaii I remember how my brothers, sister and I would lie down for our naps or go to sleep at night we would lovingly touch and lomi each other until we fell asleep. It was a caring and nurturing way to fall asleep. Our parents often asked me to massage their neck, shoulders, back and feet…so it was the origin of my training early on in my life on caring for others.

My memories as a young child with bouts of very bad stomach aches has me recalling times when my mother took me to receive *opu lomi* (stomach massage) from a woman healer who also gave me noni juice to drink and placed *lā'au lapa'au* (Hawaiian medicinal herbs) on my belly until the pain went away. It calmed me down so that I once again felt peaceful and well. I didn't like the taste of the juice but I drank it anyway because I was told that it was 'good for me'. I always felt much better after my treatment.

Growing up with lomi was such a great gift and I did not realize how valuable it was until I began to formally study and learned to appreciate the benefits of lomi from a new perspective of caring for myself as well as others on our journey to wholeness and harmony. I continue to be ever grateful for all I learn, especially for what lomi has provided for me in the past twenty three years of my life and also for being born and raised in Hawaii and all the valuable and wonderful lessons learned in nature and on the aina from my ohana.

Mahalo nui loa! I mua Aloha!

Kumu Ku'uipo Latonio

Kumu Penny Prior

www.hawaiianmassage.com

CHAPTER THIRTEEN

The Way of Lōkahi
Kahu Dane Kaohelani Silva
Ohana Learning Institute

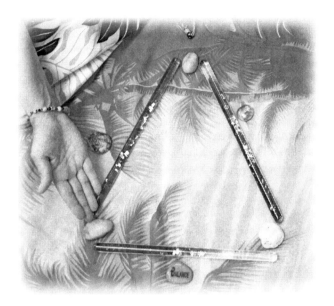

Lōkahi

The basic symbol of *Lōkahi* or unity and equilibrium is the equilateral triangle. Each side of the symbol is the same length as the other. Each corner or apex is the same angle as the other. The three corners or apices of the *Lōkahi* triangle are known as *Akua*, *Kanaka*, and *Aina*. They represent the Spirit, the Mind and the Body.

The perfect union of these three, very different aspects of the person is called *Lōkahi*. The central connection between these aspects is within the emotional center of the person. This is called the heart center of Lōkahi. The term *pu'uwai* is used to denote the emotional center of the person. The *pu'uwai* of *Lōkahi* is the heart.

Akua: Spirit

One apex of the triangle represents Spirituality. This includes the concept of *Akua* or the Creator. It also includes the concept of *Aumakua* or the ancestors. This part of the symbol called *Akua* is usually identified as the uppermost corner of the triangle. The terms grandparents, or grandfathers and grandmothers are used to remind us of the close relationships and lineage that we have with the spiritual world.

Kanaka: Mind

Another apex of the triangle represents Mankind. This includes all the people on the earth. This part of the symbol called *Kanaka* is identified as the bottom left corner of the triangle. The terms parents, or father or mother are used to remind us of the lineage within the family. The mental component of humanity is represented in this part of the triangle.

Aina: Body

The third apex of the triangle represents Nature. This includes all the living things on the earth, as well as the stones and minerals. This part of the symbol called *Aina* is identified as the bottom right corner of the triangle. The terms children, or son and daughter are used to remind us of the lineage within the family. The physical body of the human is represented in this part of the triangle.

Hā: Breath Of Life

The sides of the triangle represent the Breath. This includes the breath of life called *Hā* from the Creator, as well as from humans and plants. It also includes the air in the atmosphere.

Ola: Force Of Life

The inside of the triangle represents the energy or Life Force. This includes the nourishment that is needed to sustain the energies of mankind and nature called *Ola*.

Mana: Power Of Life

When the energy or life force accumulates and is focused through *hoʻomana* (power generation) a new apex appears above the triangle. This creates a pyramid with three sides and a base. The size of the pyramid represents the amount of *Mana* or integrated power of *Lōkahi*.

Alignment: Movement Systems

Hawaiians possess traditional ways of body movements which have been used in spiritual, martial, social and healing contexts. Ceremonies to honor the departed ancestors are marked by prayers and chants, and distinct gestures and patterns of swaying hips and motions of the arms, hands, legs and feet. Similar practices are performed for important social events within the group such as a birth, rite of passage, marriage, construction of a canoe or house, healing protocol or memorial service for a departed loved one. Each *ohana* cherishes and develops specific and unique movements that define and identify them from others within the larger community or island sectors.

Alignment: All Energy Systems

Each person requires physical or structural alignment in order to allow the smooth or maximum flow of focused energy or *mana*. This includes optimal posture, spinal and organ alignment coupled with efficient movement, circulation and breath. The healing art of lomilomi provides an effective modality for physical realignment. Physical fitness or wellness is one aspect of alignment. *Mea ʻai pono* or balanced nutrition is an essential element of the energy system. An imbalance in this system will result in sickness, disability, failure of internal organs, loss of limbs and premature death.

Mental alignment includes the understanding of one's identity. It also includes alignment of cultural and personal belief systems. It is intimately involved with family and communal relationships. Intention and visualization are coupled with breath and movement for mental fitness.

Spiritual alignment requires the physical alignment of the three main *piko* (energy centers) found in the head, the chest and the abdomen. It is functionally related to physical and mental alignment. This spiritual alignment of three different *piko* allows the optimal flow of *mana*.

The daily integration and alignment of three different culturally based concepts of body, mind and spirit comprise a balanced system of life. The study and practice of movement with breath, intention and energy flow is one traditional path to learning in this system of balance, harmony and wellness.

CHAPTER FOURTEEN

A Gift of Aloha
Kumu Michael Locey

~ The circle of life, the breath of consciousness
The divine creation of all that is
Complemented within our hearts ~ Aloha
~ Ku'uleialoha from the Aloha Messages Cards

One of the finest self-realization tools in life is to "live Aloha", and how better to do this than through lomilomi massage!

Being gifted with the *kuleana* (handed down responsibility) of lomi from my mother's tradition in Anahola, Kauai, for the last 20 years, day in and day out, hosting guests for lomi treatments "Angeline's style", I can tell you that actively participating in the Hawaiian culture (whether it be giving or receiving) connects a person to an underlying flow of Aloha spirit.

In Hawaiian culture "*mana*" is the word for energy; personal power, and it is unique to the individual. One need not worry that "power" in the sense that the world today views it is beyond ones reach because *mana* is focusing on your own individual strengths… and cultivating them.

The beauty of *aloha*, which means "standing in the presence of the divine breath", is that it is freely given and received. Becoming a Lomi practitioner is not as daunting as it seems either. It starts with the simple act of giving ourselves the gift of receiving lomilomi, from others, and when we have received, we have the potential to give this gift to others.

To live *aloha* is to receive the "gift" of Hawaii in all that it offers; the sea air, the vibrations of the ocean, the call of birds in the valley forests, and more importantly the culture and its expression through the people; particularly the *kupuna* (elders) who are the link to our past collective soul. The only requisite is that you learn to truly receive… for some it is not that easy.

When Aunty Angeline began her career in Hawaiian Wellness in the 70's, at the age of 50, most had never experienced massage as a form of wellness; including the elders of her

Hawaiian community on Kauai. Like her, they likely had received some lomi as children from a grandparent, but as they lived in an era of cultural suppression (prior to the 1970 Hawaiian renaissance), fostered in part by a strong puritanical influence, they were largely cut off from the cultural gifts of their ancestors.

Starting with the *kupuna* (elders) in Anahola, Angeline (who learned from Aunty Margret Machado) became famous as a pioneer in what she called "introducing people to their body" through lomilomi; unconditional loving touch.

When a person came to Angeline's she would take them into her steam room, rub them with *pa'a kai* and *alae'ea* (sea salt and clay), rinse them and do lomilomi, all in a steam mist. After reflecting on the transformation that would happen within the person while on her table, in her hands, she called Lomilomi "open-heart surgery".

Thanks to inspired practitioners like Angeline, practically everyone today has had some bodywork; unconditional loving touch. During the years that I worked as mom's partner in lomilomi, I witnessed countless transformations of those she called "the walking wounded" – people who learned in their short but powerful encounter with the Aloha Spirit through Angeline's hands, how to love themselves.

Cultural practitioners of Hawaiian lomilomi know that spirituality is the most important aspect. It is a powerful tool for self-realization and facilitates transformation in others.

Through prayer, meditation, visualization, *oli* (chanting), we set the intention, in harmony with the vibration of "*mauli ola*" (the source of life), and then bring it to life in the act of lomilomi.

Aunty Angeline Locey

Aunty Angeline with Ku'uleialoha

CHAPTER FIFTEEN

Talk Story with Kumu Harry Uhane Jim

Author, Wise Secrets of Aloha

~ There is no obstacle that can prevent you from moving forward
When the force is within you ~ Ho'okele

~ Ku'uleialoha from the Aloha Messages Cards

The simple story I am about to share is a tale of my work in Puna, on the Big Island of Hawaii.

Many years ago I learned Bone Washing from many of the lomi *kupuna*. Most of what I witnessed as a child was considered a common tool and technique amongst the collective of lomilomi practitioners.

It is not like massage at all. The idea in lomilomi is lifting or clearing negative memory, physical or emotional pain. This is done by using the breath, our *Hā*, touching through circular movements and tapping as we direct the energy of the memory out of the body.

Bone washing is an approach that includes the balance of breath, touch and intention while holding the space and focusing on the concept of the authority of the spiral, best understood, like the water draining in the sink. This law of gravity is present in both giver and receiver. The process of cellular release is animated and the result is phenomenal!

I hope my story will allow you to tap into the principles of my work. It has certainly made it easier, almost child's play, to work with the toughest of complaints for recurring pain.

Devon, a 14 year old, hurt his arm pitching for a high school game. His mom and dad thought his season was over. They told me Devon was unable to grasp a ball, wind it up with force and push it over home plate.

I asked Devon to sit down and asked his mom to leave us in private, so only the men were in the room.

I instructed Devon to take a deep breath from his tummy, breathing in his nose and out his mouth. 30 breaths, I instructed.

In the meantime, I chatted with his father about other therapies that they may have tried. He informed me that they tried the neighborhood chiropractor twice a week. The chiropractor told them that Devon would not be able to play baseball this season and may never recover from the wound to the soft tissue.

The dad, in his anger, "Bull shet". I ask the dad to "Flush that" feeling, sternly, as I don't need conflicting energies for the success of my treatment with his son.

The father asked "what are you going to do?" In a gentle voice, I explained that it has already started.

Devon had now completed his breathing with full effort, when I said to start over. "Why?", he asked exhausted.

The breath sets the cycle for moving the blood chemistry from acid to alkaline, I explained. No healing is done in an acid state. Lomilomi practitioners work with the body in an alkaline state, I explained, similar to the dream state.

When touching his right hand, I noticed the tips of his fingers were heavy and I suggested that he consider pushing his breath out of his index finger. He began to focus with his breath, complying as he pushed the energy out of his finger.

The dad signaled to me that he was ready for a cigarette. "Stay here, please. It is important for you to help. Devon must have your witness as he releases this wound", I requested.

We prepare the body with breath and breath only.

I began with his scapula, creating small circles lightly around the bone and parting the muscles with tapping. The muscle tension began to lift and he felt the energy running down his hand.

I asked his dad to help. By pulling his son's finger easily, the index finger . The one he was pushing his breath into.

"Oh wow", he said, "What am I feeling in his hand?"

"The tension", I explained, "is energy and it is coming from his diaphragm."

His dad still did not understand why he was holding his son's finger. I asked "Do you have something else or better to do? Now, focus on Devon and wish him better".

I moved past the scapula and penetrated, through my touch, around his deltoid muscle. Devon asked what was happening. I said, "You feel happy! You were led to believe this was a painful healing process, now flush that out with your breath and release that belief".

As Devon continued to focus with his breath, I found other spaces that I was drawn to. I tapped on the bone gently and lightly pushed on the soft tissue all the way through his tricep, past the elbow, past the wrist .I kept tapping, while spreading open the joints in his forearm.

Dad was getting excited and wanted his cigarette break and asked if he could go. "Breathe deep" I say, "there is enough nicotine in your lungs to hold this space".

"Hold space?" he said. "I don't know what that is?"

"Oh, it means you show up with your attention and choice".

By now I have tapped down and through the wrist bones and the washing was complete. The blockage at T3 was released as well. The hand felt better. I asked Devon to stand up and tap on the wall, while he claimed back his arm as a part of him that is well without strain or pain.

Devon exclaimed, "The hand is better!" His dad said, "thank you" and I said, "thank you, Devon may come back if he has another issue, but this one is done".

So friends, did you see it? It is a matter of focus and creating the drain for the stress energy to create alkalinity.

In the last three decades I've seen the community of lomilomi expand to where there are more non-hawaiian born practicing lomilomi. This is absolutely Bodacious! I'm excited to be a part of the Hawaiian healing community and join you in your passion to serve.

~ Aloha, Harry.

CHAPTER SIXTEEN

The Forgiveness Prayer
Nancy Kahalewai, LMT

~ The possibilities are limitless
where freedom is in all that is ~ Kala

~ Ku'uleialoha from the Aloha Messages Cards

Forgiveness is one of the most difficult yet liberating acts we can practice. This Forgiveness Prayer is a very precious and powerful tool. I have used it many, many times during my lomi massage sessions with amazing results. It is a perfect way to prepare for a massage, as well as a way to get beyond whatever 'stuff' may be in the moment, blocking the way to higher understanding and deeper peace. It is more powerful than its simplicity reveals, and when spoken/sent out with sincerity, I have found it to be like a 'magic carpet' that can take both practitioner and client into new and receptive places … far above and beyond our current dramas, traumas, worries and challenges.

We must remember, true forgiveness is not about lowering yourself before anyone else, or letting anyone who has hurt you / your loved ones / humanity 'off the hook'. It is potentially much more sacred. Forgiveness doesn't mean that you deny the other person's responsibility for hurting you, and it doesn't minimize or justify the wrong. As Oprah wrote on her blog, "Forgiveness doesn't mean you condone the behavior or, in any way, make a wrong right. It just means you give yourself permission to release from your past—and step forward with the mud of resentment cleared from your wings. Fly!"

As it turns out, it is actually a tool for personal liberation, because it is about letting go. But in order to truly let go, we must cultivate a certain sense of trust in the Universe and its Mysterious ways. "The great Mystery" Uncle Robert Keliihoomalu used to call it, with a smile on his aging, gorgeous Hawaiian face. He, unlike me, was truly comfortable with the great Mystery, where I (truth be told) would so prefer to analyze and understand it! But not so with Robert, as he could look up into the stars and totally surrender as he held his pearl prayer beads in his huge hands. During my years with him, he was predictably patient and grounded, and held an amazing amount of inner peace and love in his being.

Another Hawaiian elder gave my friend Daniel and I this forgiveness prayer specifically to share with our lomi students. It is short, yet very deep. A professor at the University of Hawaii at Hilo, Dr. Silva understands the Hawaiian language and all its subtle inner meanings. It goes like this:

E hui kala mai   (I extend my forgiveness)

a E hui kala aku.   (You extend your forgiveness)

(Note: repeat both lines 3x. During a massage, do it in the beginning while you place your two hands on your client/friend.)

E hui kala kakou   (We extend our forgiveness (to everyone)

Kekahi I Kekahi.   (One by One (to each and every one).

Now for more about the meaning: *HUI* means us, together; *KALA* is forgiveness. Thus together we seek and acknowledge a state of forgiveness between us. This intention is where the power lies, and must be held in one's heart and shared as such.

Wow! So let's take a deep breath, and hear this prayer deeply. "I extend my forgiveness" is different from "I forgive you". It is deeper. It means that I hold nothing against or upon you, consciously or unconsciously. I release you (and your relations/ancestors) from any and all possible issues and grievances, IF (or not) I have ever hurt or offended you (or your ancestors) in any way whatsoever. And furthermore, I acknowledge and accept your forgiveness in the same way.

The second line clears the other person (or their ancestors) from any thoughts or issues that he/she may be holding (consciously or unconsciously) towards us or our own actions, families' and ancestors.

Thus, the first two lines help clear the massage session energies between giver and receiver, and set in place healthy and sacred boundaries, as well. This is very cleansing in the massage room, but also anywhere and everywhere, as there are now no unwanted transference of energies; no *pilikia* (trauma, drama, troubles and negative stuff). That feels very *pono* (truthful) to me; how about you??!

This prayer can be chanted, spoken, or recited silently ... whatever seems most appropriate. It opens the doors for insights, intuition, and compassion to show us another level of reality. It also protects us from transference of negative energies as well, something that is vital in lomi lomi massage.

I remember clearly when Uncle Robert said a similar version of this *pule* (prayer). He would say, "If I ever did or said anything that hurt you in any way, I am very sorry." I dare say that 99% of the time there was absolutely no cause for it; it was just his way to continually maintain peace. It was amazing to witness. For to him, as well as most of the elders who mentored me, the current issues/concerns, etc. did not really matter. For it truly was all in the Creator's hands, and this prayer can release us from being entangled in it all. Forgiveness is all in the Moment, in our sincere heart's intentions!

For healing to occur, it is essential to accept forgiveness and freedom into your own heart. Otherwise, you are simply holding yourself back from what you ultimately deserve.

And, as we no doubt realize, it is not just about 'us' (you and me) but about many beings, including our families and all those whom we have crossed paths with in our lives, in the past, present, and future. Thus the last two sentences:

We extend our forgiveness to ALL / Everyone! Time to take another breath!!! Who does 'everyone' include in your Life?

And just to make sure we have not forgotten or skipped over anyone, *kekahi i kekahi* … one by one or each and every one!

No stones unturned, folks. No holding back. It is Time to LOVE and shift. Or "get over it" as Kumu Maka'ala would say. Whatever it is/was, whatever challenges/pain/issues/difficulties/heartbreaks … etc. "Just get over it." Release it! Release others, and most importantly, release yourself too!! And then sit back and watch the blessings flow.

www.bigislandmassage.com

Nancy Kahalewai

CHAPTER SEVENTEEN

Healing With Shells

Kumu Karen Leialoha Carroll

Our souls are part Mermaid, basking on deserted shores, and frolicking in deep turquoise oceans! Is it not a wonder that we love seashells? The shells whisper tales of distant places known only to our hearts, where we are free to be who we really are. The hissing of the surf is held captive in these shells, that sing the song of the ocean forever!

Kumu Karen Leialoha Carroll

As a child, I collected shells because they were little gifts left by Hina, the Goddess of the Ocean. She would leave these exquisite gifts at my feet, and I just picked them up and put them in my pocket, assured that these gifts from the ocean would always be there for me. Each shell seemed to speak to me. Like pieces of a puzzle, they were so overjoyed to be re-connected to other shells, and shared secret stories of their adventures!

I was a mer-child, loving the water so much and going the the beach with my Hawaiian Tutu (grandmother) and Chinese Kung Kung (grandfather.) If I couldn't be in the water, then I was a Mermaid on land; splashing in rain puddles and falling into fountains!

It wasn't until years later when I lived in a sacred *heiau* (Hawaiian temple) on the shores of Waimanalo Beach that I learned to use my shells to assist in healing. The home was magical, with an open atrium in the middle of the house that was screened in. When it rained outside, it also rained inside the house in the sacred garden. It was there that I reconnected to my Hawaiian culture, like the reunited seashells on the beach. There was so much to catch up with, and banquets of spiritual and sacred work to feast on! It was during this time, living on the windswept beaches of Waimanalo that I learned to hear the messages of Spirit. It was all around me, speaking to me, and giving me treasured secrets and ancient wisdom. The home was a gathering place of the highest spiritual energy, and for once, I was in the right place at the right time! This was the beginning of my spiritual journey, and I was on a crash course with destiny! Within this beautiful garden I could see and hear the unfolding of the past, where thoughts were brought to my attention, and truths revealed. Healers from all over the world showed up, uninvited, on my doorsteps. Amuah from Germany, Gen from Japan, Kahu from New Zealand, and a bevy of doctors, nurses, *Kahuna*, shaman, and *Kupuna* (elders) from Hawaii and the World! There was even a healer from Finland who agreed to receive my Lomilomi massage during a demonstration I was doing. In the blink of an eye he dropped all his clothing on the floor and was butt-naked on my table, much to the delight of my female students! It was an exciting time!

As I received the messages of spirit regarding the ancient ways, I was also taught the art of healing with shells. There was no physical teacher to teach me, but I was taught from the soul level by one who loved the ocean and shells as much as I did. Lovingly I was taught to communicate with the shells, to recognize the purpose for each one, and to be open to receive guidance in using them. The Lomilomi massage that I did, now took on an added dimension. During the Lomilomi sessions I was able to perceive what it was that my client needed for the healing of his body. Blocked energy in his forearm, disconnection of a nerve, layer upon layer of stress induced tension in his shoulders, tightness in his legs from hiking.

As I found the blockage, the shells showed me how to release the tension and pain. It was so easy, even a child could do it! The results were amazing! Even I was amazed! Tight shoulders that normally required a good 10 minutes to loosen, were now loosened in 1 minute! Completely, and without much effort! My clients raved about the results, and I couldn't believe it! There were instant results far above and beyond what I ever had dreamed was possible! It was gentle; no deep tissue massage needed, just a Lomilomi massage along with an arsenal of Shell Power to give me the edge!

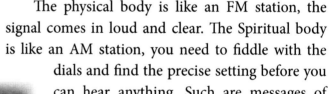

The physical body is like an FM station, the signal comes in loud and clear. The Spiritual body is like an AM station, you need to fiddle with the dials and find the precise setting before you can hear anything. Such are messages of spirit, you need to really listen, and what you listen with is not your ears. You listen with your heart. When you listen with your heart, you don't have to listen for the message anymore. You ARE the message. Everything is understood because it is a part of you. An example of this is your dog that needs to go out to potty. He relays the message to you,

"I need to go out now!" You get his message and take him out. If you ARE the dog, you don't need to relay the message, you most definitely know it!

Shells communicate from a place of knowingness. You perceive what the problem may be and they become the means to make it happen. They are shapeshifters, becoming the tool that is needed, even if that particular tool does not as yet, exist! If there are layers of stress sitting on someone's shoulders, the scooper shell becomes the shovel, or earth-mover to clear it out. If there is a knot in a runners calf, the Cowery shell turns into a magnet that pulls it all out. The muscle, now relieved of the tension, is once again soft. Because energy has weight, the shell becomes physically heavier. There is a measurable difference in weight between the "before" shell and "after" shell. The shell needs to release this energy, and placing it in a bowl of Hawaiian sea salt does exactly that.

Each shell has a purpose, if you don't know their purpose, just ask them! Being used in healing work delights them because they are fulfilling their highest good, and that is to serve unselfishly. They are living tools and even possess distinct personalities that endear them to you like a beloved pet. Some are diva shells and only want to be admired for their beauty, but don't want to work. However, most are as happy as a little clam if they have the opportunity to serve, and are faithful and skillful tools of healing.

Once I went to a flea market and was called over to a small box sitting on a table. It was as if someone took my hand and steered me over to that table. I lifted the cover and found several lovely shells. They called me because they wanted to be used to do healing work! Have you ever wanted to be chosen to do something, and were beside yourself with excitement? That is how excited shells are to be used! They will also direct you to use the shell best suited for the purpose you seek.

Shells are magical tools that know your intent. If you want them to scrape and clear the layers, think it, and it is done. You want to have the shell pull out the tension, then think it. Do you want the same shell to send healing energy to flood the area with light? Just think it, and it is done. No surgeon was ever blessed with intricate tools that perceived the doctor's intent then shape-shifted to become the tool that was needed. The shells are honored to do this work and to serve with love. In the ancient Hawaiian way, it is believed that all things are made from atoms of intelligence. We can communicate with nature, a flower, even a shell. The atoms of intelligence within it can send and receive messages. Nature has no problem doing this, it is we, who are human beings that have difficulty understanding it. When we are open to this subtle form of communication we have opened a door to fascinating new experiences.

Shells work not only on muscle tissue, they work on vital organs, nerves, and wherever there is pain and an imbalance in the body.

I once use my shells to clear symptoms of bronchitis in a young woman's lungs, they have been used to clear out toxins from an elderly man's kidneys, then charged his kidneys up with new vibrant energy. His friend was able to see the difference in him immediately! One of the things I love using the shells for, is to help with stiff arms that have difficulty lifting. Breathing the *Hā* (sacred breath), I use the scraper shell to loosen all the tightness and calcium deposits. Next, I use the Cowery to vacuum up the tension, then reverse it to send pure, clear energy into the area. A spiral shell can be used like a screw driver to loosen the joint and to lubricate it. All the work is done on the spiritual body, which is the blueprint for the physical body. What is changed in the spiritual body is changed in the physical body. You don't touch them at all with the shells, healing with shells is energy work with a tangible tool.

This is joyful work, a magical and fulfilling work. Come to think of it, it isn't work at all! Learning to use shells for healing will amaze you! You will never be able to pass another shell without whispering to it, "Hi, how are 'ya 'doin?"

www.kapuaokalani.com

Kumu Karen and Ku'uleialoha

CHAPTER EIGHTEEN

Ola ke Oli

Kumu Leilani Kalilimoku Kaleiohi

Quietly she walks upon a most sacred place on Kaua'i where her family and generations before them lived. She recalls a song, a mele, taught of these sacred grounds and begins to sing what she learned. Soon her song shifts to a chant, an oli, passed on from centuries ago. Each line reveals many aspects of importance to her culture; names of the winds and the mountain peaks, of messages revealed about the stars, tides, winds, genealogy, love, history and learned ways of survival.

Appreciative of the abundance of knowledge, she gently touches the soil and foliage still thriving and feels compelled to hum additional melodic tones inspired by the specific emotional feel of the moment. Her eyes fascinated by the natural environment which surrounds her, she is innately aware of all that is sharing this special time and place with her.

She follows the practice of her family and feels the wind rustling through the foliage join in. She spots a native bird to the lands perk up to chime in with an enduring melody of his own. She pauses to giggle as she listens to his flirtatious song. She then glances up at the sky, watching the clouds' movements as they gracefully paint familiar images for her to see. Messages from the heavens speak to her of life's constant cycle and turns. She peacefully smiles at the flowing water of the stream upon the rocks as the sound sings with a melody as ancient as life itself.

New words emanate into voiced notes as her melody leads her to step further into a prayerful oli, honoring the moment. Together with nature and the elements that surround her, they chant of the experience and praise. Together a new oli with its own sacred story is born. For her, it also means that precious moment she connects with her native ancestral roots through the use of her voice that allows her to step back in time and space to be with them, to learn from and see what they saw of this beautiful place, and to voice these messages in the present. It is here she is most peaceful within, for its home to her inherited heart and soul.

To learn the art of Hawaiian Oli is to learn the language and many aspects of the culture, past and present. Oli is the telling story of a bond embedded deep within and voiced, a story of life's observances and survival familiar to indigenous peoples around the globe for centuries, and passed on from generation to generation, storyteller to storyteller.

Such is the story of our native ancestors who were among the first humans to have arrived on these lands and wrote chants in praise of what they experienced, honored, loved and treasured. Traveling across the vast Pacific Ocean in canoes, they discovered the Hawaiian Archipelago and found these islands of great beauty filled with natural resources and exceptional celestial location. Here they choose to remain and steward these precious gifts, these blessings bestowed upon them. Throughout their stay they continued to create numerous chants passing on their knowledge for generations to come.

To this day native Hawaiians continue their ancestral legacy; stewards who still live where their ancestors roamed; plant fields of food and medicine for the family upon, fish the ocean and streams, teach their children to carry on the legacies and lessons left by the ancestors, and when necessary stand firmly to protect their sovereignty.

Ola ke oli - chant lives on.....

Kumu Leilani Kalilimoku Kaleiohi

SECTION III

Earth's Healing Ceremony

Creator, I come before you in a humble manner and offer you this sacred prayer

To the four powers of creation

To the Sun and Moon, Earth and the ʻAumakua

I pray for my relations in nature

All those who walk, crawl, fly or swim

To the good spirits that exist in every part of creation

I ask that you bless our Kupuna and Keiki, ʻOhana and friends, both brothers

And sisters and those we don't know

I pray for the sick, homeless and forlorn

May there be good health and healing for all on this earth and for the earth

May there be beauty above me and all around me

I ask that this world be filled with peace and love

May your dreams be sweet

Your heart at peace

Your spirit be filled with fire for a new tomorrow

Amama ua noa

"Never assume a message is just for you
Messages are a divine unfolding process
that we as humans may not fully understand.
Once we move past the ego and open our heart,
only then will we comprehend."

~ *Ku'uleialoha*

A massage is emotional, mental, spiritual
before it is physical.
~ *Kumu Alva Andrews*

THE LOMILOMI SESSION

The outline you will find on the following pages is a **guide** only. It is not in a sequence format for a specific reason. It is not intended to teach you a protocol of technique.

Lomilomi is a 'guided' session and may include many modalities. It will also vary from each client and each session. The body is never the same.

Lomilomi can be performed on a mat, in a chair or on a massage table. Lomilomi can even be performed in the water. There are no limits to where it can be applied as it is about the intention and not the technique.

Remember

1. Every lomi session begins with *pule*.
2. Lomi practitioners may use an *oli* (chant) or *pule* handed down by their *kumu*.
3. Lomi practitioners may also include herbal medicines.
4. Let your intuition be your guide.
5. Always honor their sacred space.

As you open your *pu'uwai* to learning about your journey, your purpose and providing the compassionate touch through the love of ke Akua; I invite you to continue your studies. This is only an introduction to the profound healing that Lomilomi can provide you and your clients.

"The kahuna view the human physical body as an intensely energized thought form... For the healing to take place, the paths that the energies follow in our lives must be open. The "path" or the "light" are all symbolic terms used to describe the ways of connection between the Lower Self and Higher Self."

~ Sondra Ray

CLEARING

OPENING

Lomilomi does not always begin with massage. You might find traditional practitioners providing a steam, salt scrub and other herbal coaching prior to the actual bodywork. Once a client comes to the table, the lomi practitioner may be clearing energetic blockages to prepare the body for the actual massage. Depending on the training one might have it could include a combination of energetic techniques, including polarity, cranio sacral etc. In some 'ohana they believe you clear from the crown of the head and others believe the feet need to be cleared to release stagnate energy or exhaust.

1. Connect with your client and evaluate their breathing. Notice where they are holding their breath.

   We want to create movement in their body, especially along the spine where the nerves reside and assist in the function of the whole body.

2. If you are trained to read their cranio sacral rhythm or the flow of the cerebrospinal fluid (CSF) you can also apply those skills

3. You can begin prone or supine.

1. Begin by clearing the energy down the body and out of the feet.

2. You might also apply some gentle rocking techniques, similar to Trager.

3. Using your intuition while you are evaluating the energy, you might be using acupressure points or compression holds.

4. Pause and allow the body to assimilate the new space.

5. Reevaluate and repeat as necessary.

1. Shake or vibrate the foot, loosening all the muscles and creating more space between the tarsal bones.

2. Continue with long sweeping strokes down the body and off the feet.

3. Use gentle rocking as needed.

4. Pause

(I like to think of this process as clearing and creating space so that the muscles have a new place to set once you begin your massage)

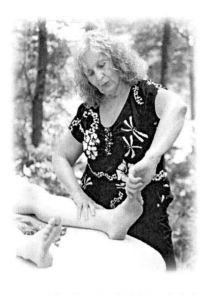

1. When clearing the legs and feet remember to take the energy right through and off the toes.

2. Rock the legs gently, following the movement of the body. Don't push the body into a space. Recognize where the body is living in this moment.

3. Listen and follow the movements gently creating new space.

Gentle stretches at the joints will also help open and clear blockages. Feel how far the body wants to move into these spaces, without pushing too hard.

1. Evaluate the energy.

2. Pause and hold. Allow the client a chance to assimilate into the new space.

Remember to continually clear using your Hā breath

When clearing the energy of your client, you might find this could take 5 minutes or 50 minutes. It all depends on the condition of their body and the state of their well being. Don't rush the process. Your client will feel very relaxed during this process.

CHAPTER TWENTY

DRAPING

I would like to address the concern of draping in this chapter.

One of the biggest controversies I have seen amongst lomilomi practitioners and kumu, is the draping styles. Personally, I drape according to my client's comfort level and I don't believe that only one way is the right way. Typically, the draping methods you learned in Swedish massage will most often be used with some modifications occasionally.

Keep in mind it is crucial for your client to feel safe, no matter what draping style you prefer to use in your lomilomi sessions.

Long Forearm Strokes require more freedom to perform the technique and you might find more limited draping in this case.

PRONE DRAPING

Method 1
In this method of draping, you can begin by draping with the sheet on an angle and adding a small towel to create more comfort and security.

* The back will remain undraped so that a long flowing forearm stroke can be applied completely down the body.

Method 2

In this style of limited draping, the client is draped with a smaller towel. I like to firmly press the towel or pillow case against the legs, so the client feels secure.

The client must be comfortable with this method as well as the practitioner.

Obviously it allows for more freedom of performing your techniques. However, it can also be questionable for those that are inhibited or uncomfortable.

CAUTION: Please always make sure you use appropriate draping that makes your client comfortable. It is about them.

Method 3

In this method of draping the back is exposed. We can tuck the sheet under the leg as in the photo. The angle by the hip allows for access to the hip and freedom for longer strokes.

Method 4

Keep the drape tucked and secure as in the photo.
The legs are covered and kept warm, while the back is being addressed.

Method 5

Most clients are comfortable remaining draped on one side while you massage the other side.

Drape the client with a towel when performing the abdominal techniques.

When performing abdominal techniques (Opu Huli), you can drape as in this photo.

You may prefer to tuck your drape under the arms as in the photo. This will allow you freedom to access the shoulder and chest without the drape getting in the way.

Keep in mind no matter what style of draping you prefer to utilize, always ask your client if they are comfortable. During a session if a client gets cold, drape them.

**It is always about comfort and
safety first for your client!**

CHAPTER TWENTY-ONE

PREPARATION

PULE

Lomilomi always begins with *pule* (prayer). We ask for divine guidance, wisdom and protection from *ke Akua*. Set your intention for the healing to take place, non-verbally. We ask that the recipient be willing to receive.

Pule may be done during a session as well and upon completion. We give thanks and gratitude at completion.

Take your time and breathe with your client.

CONNECTING & BREATHING

This also gives the practitioner time to connect with their client energetically. Your client may find this comforting as well.

If you are trained in cranio sacral therapy, you might read the rhythm at this time.

Begin entering the etheric space above the body slowly and respectfully. Pay attention to the breathing patterns. Feel the energy above their body. Pay attention to their breath. As they inhale allow your hand to meet their body. This is a gentler, non-invasive way to connect with your client.

I *always* inform my students to imagine they have a cranky baby they are trying to put to sleep at 3a.m. How would you touch them, move or nurture them?

LUBRICANTS

Traditionally, coconut and/or kukui nut oil was used because that is what is available on the islands. Lomilomi, however, was also performed fully clothed and for some 'ohana (family), there was no use of lubrication. Some might perform a more energetic type of work first and when they felt the body was prepared and ready for the massage , they would use the oil.

Today we have a variety of creams, oils and lotions. I would choose a natural, preferably organic, product. Some companies even make creams infused with coconut oil.

UNDRAPING

Every movement and every touch should always be performed extremely consciously and cautiously, even draping.

Begin by barely allowing your client to feel the movement of the sheet or your hands and move very slowly.

I will demonstrate beginning our session in the prone position.

Bring the drape down to the lower back and create an angle along the side of the hip for best access to perform your forearm stroke.

1. We breathe the *Hā* breath into the oil to bring *'ola* (life force) into our oil.

2. Begin by applying our oil to the palm of our hand and on our forearm.

3. Slowly and gently, working with the breath, we begin to apply the lubricant with our forearm.

Using your forearms with gentle strokes, your client will begin to relax with with these nurturing strokes. Hypnotize your client into relaxation.

REMEMBER: Most people are stressed or in pain. The parasympathetic nervous system is often overly stressed and not functioning optimally. It is through this gentle touch that we encourage the parasympathetic nervous system to relax the body, mind and spirit.

CHAPTER TWENTY-TWO

THE FOREARM TECHNIQUE

APPLICATION AND MECHANICS

The forearm technique is one of the most popular strokes in the Temple style lomilomi. It is also a great technique that will save your wrists and hands from stress. The strokes will be long, fluid and graceful. The forearm technique is also a wonderful integrative stroke during your treatment.

With the correct body mechanics and hand placement this technique creates a feeling of an ocean wave that blesses the cells. Lomi students learn how to properly perform this technique through vigorous lua (martial arts) and other movement exercises.

1. Begin by bending your knees and positioning the side of your hand as in the photo. Start with the side of your fingers slicing through the tissue at approximately the level of C-6 "across" the cervical and trapezius musculature. Your hand, wrist and forearm all fully engaged, gliding through. As you approach midway, your forearm will be in an upright position. Your body lifts as you follow the movement.

2. Make sure you are going across the musculature and not sliding down the trapezius. Your body will be moving from a slight squat to upright position, following your hand and arm movement.

(3a)

3. Once you are mid way with your forearm as in the photo (3a)...

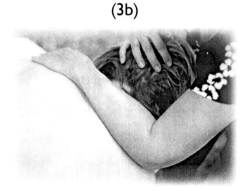

(3b)

4. Relax your arm across the upper back (3b). The hands and wrists are always straight and aligned, loose, relaxed and with no fists.

5. Begin to glide down the erector spinae with a firm and focused touch with the one arm and allow the other hand to support the body. (Once you become proficient with this move, the other hand can be applying another technique). Imagine that you are water and it is flowing down their back.

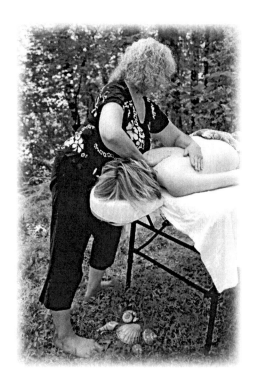

CHAPTER TWENTY-THREE

BASIC BACK TECHNIQUES

Most clients love their back massaged!

By creating a soothing and relaxing session you can provide a space for the parasympathetic nervous system to take your client into deeper places of serenity.

Begin by slowly entering the body allowing your hands to meld with your clients breath.

NOTE: Be mindful of cold hands touching their body. This is not soothing and often shocks your client. Pay attention to the temperature of your hands and how you initially touch their skin.

1. Begin with 3 strokes down the back, up and around the sides of the body, through their shoulders and back down.

2. As your arms come back up through the sides, allow your forearms to sink into the crease of the shoulder joint and gently compress

3. Slide back and forth with your forearms, opening this joint space.

4. As your arms come through, allow your hands to shift position down and come through the trapezius and cervical region.

5. Clear the energy. Use your Hā Breath.

6. Repeat these strokes 3 times.

CLEARING THE SPINE - also called *WIGGLY WIGGLY*

1. Place your index finger and middle finger along side the spine on the erector spinae.

2. Place your opposite hand on top of the bottom hand.

3. As you glide down along the spine, gently stretching the erectors, your top hand creates a vibration or wiggly movement back and forth.

4. Repeat 3 times.

FOREARM STROKE

1. Continue with your forearm stroke as described previously.

2. Connect with the tissue firmly and allow yourself to be received by the body.

3. Adjust your pressure accordingly when the tissue softens.

4. This stroke should not start out heavy. The intention is to open, clear and relax the muscles first.

5. Perform these long strokes for approx 10 minutes or until your client has relaxed.

Note: The limited draping allows for easier flow down the full body.

6. This stroke can continue all the way down the back of the leg creating one long fluid stroke.

CLEARING SUBSCAPULARIS

1. As in the photo bring your forearm up against (but not on) the scapula.

2. By changing the angle of your ulnar you can access more specifically.

3. By lifting your arm up, you can change the depth of pressure as needed. Use caution.

4. Your range of motion movements can be applied here.

Repeat with several long forearm strokes in between each technique. Clear and release the energy.

Once the spine is relaxed you can now address it from the side angle.

1. Place your hands in a relaxed position as in the photo.

2. Align your thumbs alongside the erector spinae.

3. Gently push medially and glide upward. Repeat 3 times.

4. Perform a long fluid forearm stroke to provide the body with an integrated feeling .

5. Focus on regions that need attention.

6. Combine techniques that you are feeling called to apply. For example: Trigger point therapy, myofascial release, cranio sacral therapy or other structural type of work.

REMEMBER! The session is guided by the client and the wisdom you are receiving from the 'Aumakua.

CAUTION: Resist having an agenda when treating. Listen more attentively to create space and provide the loving touch through the techniques the clients are ready to receive.

UPON COMPLETION OF THE BACK

1. Cover the client's body with ease and grace keeping in mind they are deeply relaxed.

2. Apply some clearing strokes over the sheets.

3. Breathe and release. Do not hold onto any residual energy you might have taken on. Let it go.

CHAPTER TWENTY-FOUR

CERVICAL TECHNIQUES

The cervical muscles love lomilomi! Remember, everything you know about massage is included in lomilomi. Integrate your Swedish massage techniques!

1. Massage the neck to warm up the tissue.

2. Gently compress and lift while you stretch apart as in the photo.

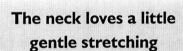

The neck loves a little gentle stretching

2. Repeat 3 times and follow up through the occiput. Complete with some effleurage.

1. Place the pad of your thumb along the ridge of the occiput. Start at the center and move along the ridge laterally.

2. Apply gentle pressure and slightly lift superior. *Think Create space.*

3. Allow the pressure to increase only if the muscle tissue is softening.

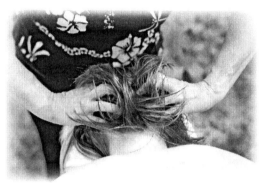

4. Repeat on both sides.

5. Finish with a scalp massage.

When your client is ready to turn supine, be sure to have them properly draped. Make sure they are warm enough and comfortable.

NOTE: You may want to see if they need a bathroom break before you begin supine.

SUPINE NECK TECHNIQUES

Supine Neck techniques are similar to Swedish massage.

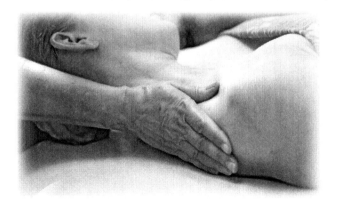

1. Scoop around the trapezius and through the neck several times.

2. Gently and slowly lift the head off the table.

3. Clear out the cervical muscles along side of the spine by gliding with the pad of your thumb from the occiput down through the trapezius junction.

4. Repeat and clear 3 times.

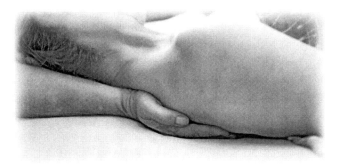

5. Place the palm of your hand under the scapula and sweep from the back up through the trapezius and through the neck.

6. With the pads of your finger tips glide up and through the neck superior.

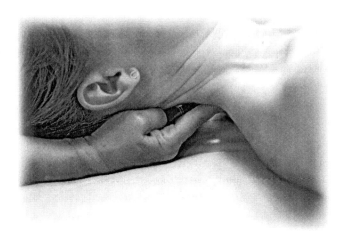

7. Take your fingertips through the scalp and off the head. Repeat these actions 3 times.

8. Range of motion as described in Chapter 21.

9. Finish with long flowing strokes through the chest, around the shoulders and neck . Proceed into the face techniques.

Check in with your client as needed to make sure they are comfortable.

RANGE OF MOTION

Lomilomi always includes the clearing of the joints or range of motion.

Kumu Harry Uhane explains in his book *"Wise Secrets of Aloha"*, that the Hawaiians saw the periosteum, the skin of the human bone, as the cache where memory was stored. Encouraging the stagnant energy to be cleared from the muscle tissue will create more fluidity and flexibility.

In this chapter you will find a variety of positions to create space and increase the range of motion. It can be equated to washing or clearing the bones through a gentle, non-invasive rocking and vibration.

Here are examples of various positions to create space and increase range of motion in the prone and supine positions at the joint spaces.

Apply similar movements to all joints during your lomilomi session as you see fit for each client.

SHOULDER JOINT – PRONE POSITION

1. Gently lift the joint. Feel the weight in all directions.

2. Rock slowly and notice how it feels, how it moves.

3. Patiently allow the rocking or shaking motion to free up the joint space, creating more space.

4. Follow the movement further into the range of motion.

Chapter Twenty-Five *Range Of Motion* 107

1. From the opposite side, gently place your hands under the shoulder as seen in the picture.

2. Feel the weight of the shoulder as you slowly lift and release.

3. Notice how it feels? Where does it move? Where is it holding?

4. Begin to slowly move the scapula in circular movements, paying attention to how it moves.

   Pause and relax. Repeat in the opposite direction.

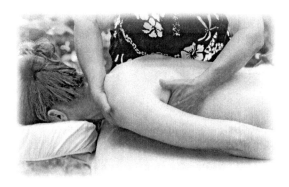

5. Move the scapula in the opposite direction and repeat slow movements in a circular pattern.

   Pause and relax.

6. Repeat several times, noticing the movement of the scapula. Are the movements getting fuller? Is the shoulder getting lighter? Is energy releasing?

7. Follow the movements slowly into the positions where they want to move. Hold, wait and release.

1. Reposition your hands as in the photo (a). With your thumbs along the spine of the scapula gently sink into the tissue.

2. Gently rock, shake and vibrate.

3. Rotate the scapula in small circular movements from this angle.

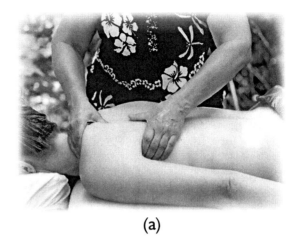

(a)

4. As the tissue opens and releases your thumbs should sink into the muscle along the spine. If this happens, create a gentle stretch in the space. as in the second photo (b). Repeat.

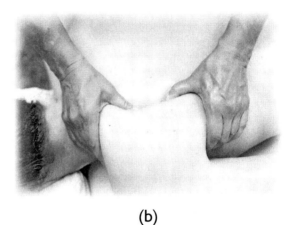

(b)

1. Hold the arm upward. Follow it through. Take the arm through a slower range of motion. Pay attention to where you might feel any blockages or restrictions.

2. Wiggle, shake, vibrate the energy to clear the space . Repeat as necessary.

3. Repeat the R.O.M. in both directions (clockwise and counter clockwise).

4. Rock the arm capsule gently. Notice how it feels, how it moves. Repeat as necessary.

5. Apply a gentle stretch and combine with R.O.M. and long flowing strokes/effleurage to the forearm. These combined strokes feel wonderful!

CERVICAL REGION - SUPINE POSITION

1. Gently caress the cervical musculature without pulling the neck.

2. Place a small amount of tension along the cervical spine . Do not pull. (a)

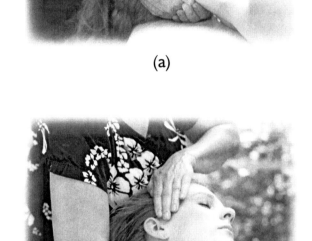

(a)

3. Slowly move the neck into new spaces. Evaluate the tissue, the movements and the restrictions.
   Ask your client to breath.
   Hold and release.

   Slowly bring to center. Pause
   Repeat on the opposite side.

4. Place your hands as shown in picture (b)

(b)

5. Lift the head slightly and allow the cervical muscles to rest on your forearm. One hand rests on the shoulder and one on the head as demonstrated in the photo.

6. Slowly follow the movements.

7. Have your client breathe into the spaces and hold for a cycle of 3 breaths.

8. Slowly Release and repeat.
   Perform on both sides 3 times.

9. Bring the head back to center slowly.

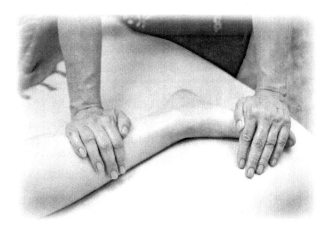

1. Gently move the ankle as far as it will comfortably position for your client in a lateral position. Hold for a few seconds and gently release.

2. Allow foot to come back to neutral position.

NOTE: Always check in with your client prior to performing and make sure they have no ankle issues or contraindications.

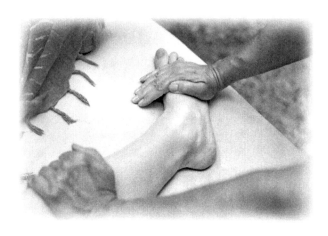

3. Reverse and move the ankle gently into the medial position, support and hold. Release. Repeat several times back and forth as demonstrated in the photos.

4. Support the ankle in neutral position and slowly perform clockwise range of motion. Pause.
Repeat counter clockwise
Pause. Relax.

5. You may want to include some rocking, shaking or vibration to relieve any tension in this region.

1. Place your hands softly supporting the knee and ankle.

2. Gently lift up and off the table.

3. Rock and shake back and forth creating more space at the hip joint.

4. Rotate the knee joint laterally gently (unless of course the patient has had recent surgery or has pins to stabilize the joint). Use caution.

5. Rotate the ankle joint as long as there are no contraindications.

6. Allow for the joints to wiggle and wobble, loosening and opening slowly. Follow their pattern of movement while supporting the leg.

7. Play with the movements. Let the joints move in any direction of ease.

8. Hold in tighter spaces, ask your client to breathe.

   Release slowly.

9. Re-evaluate for lightness, motion and tissue release. Breathe your Hā breath and clear the energy.

NOTE: Whenever performing R.O.M. make sure your client has not had recent surgery.

FEET AND ANKLES – PRONE POSITION

1. Supporting the ankle and foot, gently move the joints into a slight stretch.

2. Follow the ankle and foot into the range that is comfortable for your client.

3. Shake the foot, vibrate and rock until it becomes looser.

4. Wiggle each tarsal bone and allow for the muscles to relax into the new spaces.

Note: Make sure your client's knees are comfortable. Give them position to readjust as necessary.

HIP ROTATION SUPINE

1. Position the leg as seen in the photo and your hands supporting as shown. Securely drape your client.

2. Gently guide the movement superior. Do not fully push the knee toward the body. Encourage your client to breathe.

3. Slowly rotate around the hip joint holding in tighter areas. Have your client breathe into the space. Release slowly. Continue to move around clockwise.

4. Repeat counter clockwise and come back to neutral.

5. Ask your client to take a deep breath and on the exhale gently move the knee closer to their chest and hold. Only go as far as the space was created.

6. Perform Range of motion again slowly in both directions.

7. You can also rock, shake or vibrate as necessary.

8. Return to neutral position. Supporting the leg and back of the knee bring the leg down onto the table.

9. Rock the whole leg several times. Relax and release.

CHAPTER TWENTY-SIX

LEG TECHNIQUES

PRONE TECHNIQUES

1. Using your forearm stroke apply your oil or cream with long flowing strokes.

   Repeat several times.

2. Remember to clear the energy and use your Hā breath.

3. With your forearms begin to roll and compress as you work superior. Keep your arms relaxed.

4. Increase pressure as the body is ready to receive you.

5. Integrate the long flowing forearm stroke as desired or needed.

6. Bend the knee and continue using forearm strokes up to through the hamstrings.

Note: You can sit on the table to perform this technique, if this is comfortable for you.

7. Allow the knee to move in different directions and follow through the range.

8. As you bend the knee allow it to rest on your arm or shoulder. The outside arm will continue up and through the hip with a long wave-like stroke.

As you gain more confidence and move with more ease in your body, these techniques will get easier.

9. Continue to stretch and flex the knee for a nice quad stretch.

10. Bring the forearm back down and through the hamstrings and quads.

11. Bring the leg down flat and finish with flowing strokes off and through the foot.

1. Place the leg in Tree pose (yoga) as shown in the photo.

2. Make sure draping feels secure. Tuck along the sides of the leg. You can also use a diaper type draping method here if your client prefers.

3. With your forearm gently apply compression and glide several times.

This is a favorite of my clients!

4. Bring the leg across for a nice stretch. Be sure to keep client draped appropriately.

5. Apply gentle compression and with your forearm glide through the iliotibial band. Repeat as needed.

6. Work within the tolerance and threshold of your client. Check in with your client to see if the pressure or leg positioning needs to be adjusted.

7. With the knee in a bent position, as in the photo, place your hands as demonstrated. Compress slightly as you sit back into the position. Create a nice opening and stretch through the hip and groin.

Note: Sit on the table as in the photo to perform this technique. Sitting back as you perform the technique will be much easier to apply.

8. Continue to hold the leg in this gentle stretch begin to move it slowly within the joint space. Make small circular movements.

9. With your forearms and light lubrication use your forearms to massage the leg with fluid strokes.

10. Finish with long gliding strokes and foot massage!

CHAPTER TWENTY-SEVEN

FOOT TECHNIQUES

FOOT TECHNIQUES IN THE PRONE POSITION

Rest the foot on a pillow or your leg as in the photo.

Opening the energy gates and clearing to create space is our main goal in this foot treatment

1. Beginning at the center of the heel apply gentle pressure. These points in reflexology relate to the sciatic nerve area.

2. Apply gentle pressure in a straight line down the foot to the middle toe.

3. Bring your thumb back to your starting point. Continue to compress gently down the foot again to the next toe. You will be walking through 5 zones on the bottom of the feet all ending at the toes.

**NOTE: In Thai massage the feet and legs house Sen Channels.
The spleen, liver, kidney, stomach, gallbladder and bladder.**

If you have studied reflexology you will know these points relate to all the organs of the body.

4. After all five zones have been opened, proceed to creating more space within the joints. Move the joints in different directions. Apply compression, gentle stretches or vibration.

5. Sandwich the foot between your hands as in the photo. Gently stretch the foot to each side. Repeat this procedure on both feet. 2-3 x on each foot SLOWLY.

CAUTION: If your client has had foot surgery or has pins in their foot/ankle, please avoid any twisting actions.

6. Place the palms of your hand at the side of the foot while it is in a flexed position (prone). Vibrate vigorously . This will help 'create' space and loosen the tightness in the foot.

7. Bring the foot down slowly as you clear the energy off and through the foot to the toes on both sides.

Very helpful for anyone who stands or works on their feet all day!

1. Place the foot on a pillow if needed for comfort.

2. Begin by gently shaking the leg and foot.

(BUTTERFLY FLUTTER)
   a. Place your hands under under the hamstring and through the calf.
   b. Allow your fingers to create a 'butterfly' movement as you wiggle down the leg. Repeat 3 times.

3. Apply a small amount of lubricant.

4. Gently massage into the foot.

5. Apply slow stretches in a downward direction
   a. Always check in with your client for their comfort level
   b. **NEVER** force any stretch
   c. **THINK** – Create space

6. With soft hands gently compress laterally (Eversion).
   a. Apply gentle compression on the inside of the calf. From the ankle and moving upward, apply compression. Repeat 2-3 times.

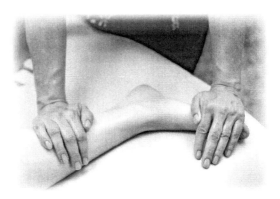

   b. SLOWLY release the foot back into a straight and natural position.

7. Repeat by placing the foot into Inversion. Apply gentle compressions while stretching as in # 6. Repeat 2-3 x. Replace foot slowly in a neutral position.

8. Massage the foot around the ankles with circular motions and through the entire foot.

9. Complete your session by wrapping warm towels around the feet for a minute. Gently compress . Ahhhh!

You can start your foot treatment with a wonderful foot soak. Place a few of your favorite essential oils in the water. Sprinkle fresh flowers in season to create a wonderful ambiance. Perform a salt scrub on the feet and calf. This feels very rejuvenating!

CHAPTER TWENTY-EIGHT

ARMS AND SHOULDER TECHNIQUES

Lomilomi of the arms is a combination of clearing the energy, range of motion, gentle stretches and Swedish type of strokes. Creating long fluid strokes that integrate the arms with the neck, shoulders and chest feel wonderful.

I. Effleurage the arm.

1. Caress the shoulder and bring gentle movement into the joint.

2. Follow back down the arm with effleurage.

3. Repeat again and then bring your hands across the chest and back as in next photo.

1. Taking your arms across the chest and under the back feels wonderful and comforting.

2. Allow your hands to continue down the arms and into their hands and fingers.

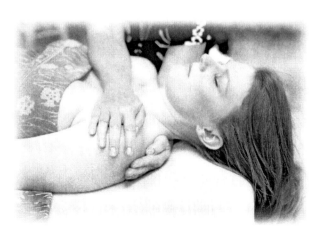

1. Perform range of motion slowly.

2. You can also include gentle rocking and shaking.

1. As you gently lift and stretch the arm you can also combine some effleurage strokes through the arm.

2. Combining the lift, stretch and movement with the strokes feels wonderful.

3. Place the arm down gently and finish with a hand massage.

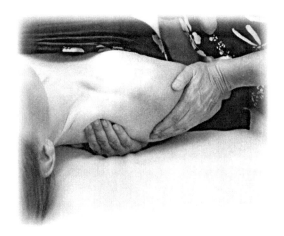

1. Bring your inside hand under the back and through the rhomboids until you can gently push through the trapezius as in the photo.

2. Alternate with your opposite hand coming from the top of the trapezius and through the rhomboids and around.

3. Create an alternating wave like movement to open the scapula.

4. Complete with effleurage down the arm and off the hands.

CHAPTER TWENTY-NINE

FACE TECHNIQUES

Face techniques are relaxing, rejuvenating and help relieve sinus pressure as well as relieving headaches.

STEP I

1. Keep hands, wrist and arms soft so the strokes can glide smoothly around the face. My secret to flowing around the face is to keep my joint relaxed in all movements.

2. Enter slowly and with arms crossed at the wrist, as in the picture. Apply the lotion or oil around and through the side of the face.

Lotion: You don't need to apply a large amount of lubrication. Make sure you inquire if your client is allergic to any types of oils, nuts, fragrances etc., before working on the face

3. Continue around the mandible as in picture #2.

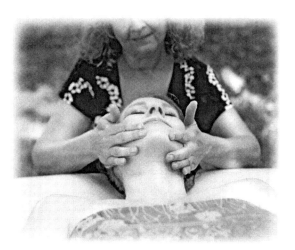

The face has many lymphatic drainage channels.

Apply lighter pressure.

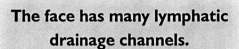

Acupressure points around sinus regions are helpful in clearing the sinus passages.

Relaxing strokes on the face are blissful!

1. Bring your hands around the crown of the head with thumbs on the frontal bone. Apply gentle pressure on the frontal bone with the pads of your thumb.

2. Gentle press superior through the midline of the frontal bone.

3. Repeat all steps 3 times.

STEP 3 - ACUPRESSURE POINTS

1. Begin along the ridge of the mandible with light pressure.

2. Follow around the jaw line squeezing gently.

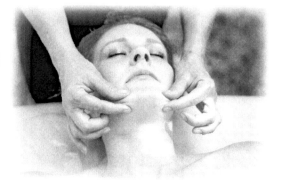

3. Place the pads of your finger tips under the zygomatic arch and apply gentle pressure.

4. Apply pressure along the sinus points out laterally. Repeat.

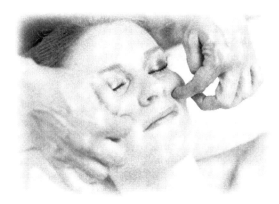

5. Continue with gently squeezing along the brow line. Begin at the midline and working out laterally.

STEP 4 - TEMPORAL LOBE COMPRESSION

1. With the palms of your hands gently squeezing as in the photo, compress lightly and release. Repeat 3x.

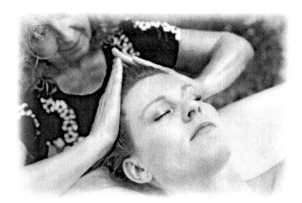

TEMPORAL LIFT

2. With your hands placed at the temporal lobe begin to compress lightly and *lift* upward as in the photo. Repeat 3 times.

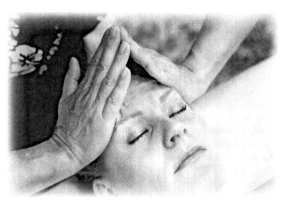

STEP 5 - EARS

1. Gently compress around the edge of the ear lobe.

   Repeat 3 times.

2. Massage the ear.

3. You can also include a scalp massage.

Go back to Step 1 and repeat the long flowing strokes around the face to complete your face sequence.

CHAPTER THIRTY

OPU HULI (to turn over)
ABDOMINAL MASSAGE

Abdominal massage is an integral part of every lomilomi session.

The abdominal region contains a huge amount of our lymphatic drainage system and our organs of process, filtration and excrement. Abdominal massage also aids in relieving back stress and aligning and integrating the body more fully.

As we perform our lomilomi massage we are continually addressing the lymphatic system through a variety of our gentler techniques. Therefore, addressing and clearing the abdominal cavity near the end of a session is extremely beneficial. In ancient times you were considered an excellent lomi practitioner when the client had a bowel movement following the session..

This is a sampling of the abdominal techniques you might perform. However, you can integrate and learn more as you study. You may also find each kumu teaches it slightly different.

Many of your clients may have never experienced an abdominal massage until now.
Always enter this space respectfully and slowly.

1. Apply a small amount of lubrication in your palms and on your forearms.

2. Begin by hovering over the client's abdomen.

3. Watch their breath. As they inhale allow their body to touch your hand. This is a non-invasive way of approaching the body and received by the client with more ease.

4. As they exhale allow your hand to sink in with the exhalation.

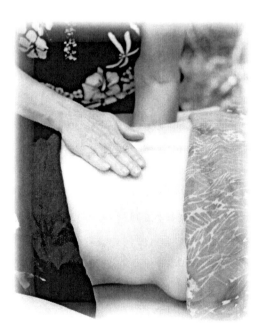

5. Place your other hand underneath their back.

6. Hold in neutral for 3 cycles of breathing. This gives your client an opportunity to feel comfortable with you in this sacred center of their life force ('ola)

7. Breathe with your client.

8. The palm of your hand is directly over the pico (naval chakra).

9. Your bottom hand is directly in alignment with your top hand.

The client is draped across the chest. This allows for enough space to perform your techniques.

1. Once you have made the connection, begin with small clockwise circles above and below, slowly. Repeat 3 times. Once for body, mind and spirit or once for the ʻāina, ʻohana and ke Akua.

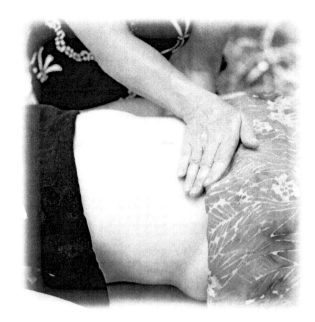

2. Next, place your hand over the piko (belly button region). Follow the breath with the exhale and gently allow your hand to sink into the abdomen. Continue to gracefully enter this sacred space and allow for the energy to open and flow.

3. Place your hands under the back and lift and shake gently – creating space through the lumbar region.

This should be performed with ease. Never try to lift someone more than the body is willing to go.

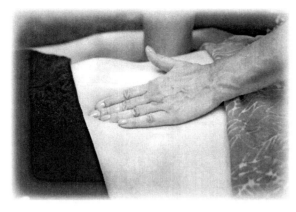

4. Place your hands at the solar plexus or diaphragm region. Follow the breath on the exhale and sink in slowly.

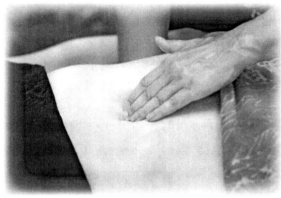

5. As you sink down (towards the table), you will gently glide down inferior to just above the belly button. Repeat this process 3 times.

6. Placing your hand on an angle just beneath the rib cage. Allow your hand to sink into this space on the exhale.

   Gently glide diagonally approx. 3 inches.

7. Reposition your hand at the starting point and working with the breath repeat 2 more times.

Continue this same procedure on the opposite side of the body. Complete with a circular (clockwise) abomdinal massage.

Clearing the abdominal region helps aid in digestion and assimilation. It is also beneficial for all the organ functions. Adominal massage is also indicated for individuals with back pain. *DO NOT*perform abdominal massage on pregnant woman. Proper training in pregnancy massage is suggested.

CHAPTER THIRTY-ONE

LOMI IN THE CHAIR

Lomilomi can be performed anywhere, even in a regular chair.

Take 10 to 15 minutes and provide loving touch to your friends, colleagues and clients.

All Lomilomi begins with Pule and compassionate touch. It is all about your intention.

Here I will provide you with a few photos illustrated techniques in the chair.

Always advise your client to focus on breathing. As they exhale apply your gentle pressure. And they inhale allow and the body rises, allow your hands or forearms to rise up and release the pressure.

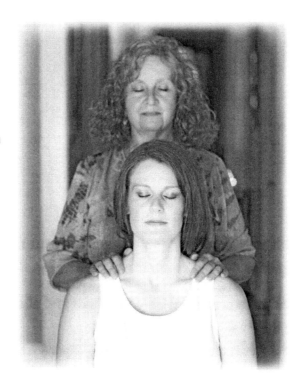

1. Set the intention.

2. Pule.

3. Gentle, compassionate touch and connect with the breath.

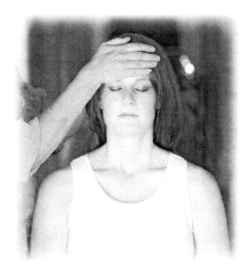

1. Place the palm of your hand on the frontal bone and the other hand on the back of the head for support.

2. Gentle Compress as as the client breathes.

3. Continue compressing across the frontal bone to each side.

1. Place the palms of your hands at the side of the skull.

2. Gently compress and lift superior as they exhale 3 times.

1. With your forearms (palms up) sink into the trapezius muscle on their exhale 3 times.

2. It helps to breathe with your client and allow for the energy to flow together.

1. With soft fists, starting beneath the occiput, roll down through the cervical muscles into the trapezius.

2. Repeat from the occiput through the trapezius 3 times as your client breathes.

3. Place your hands in the position as demonstrated in the photo. Ask your client to breathe. Gently take them into a stretch. Stop at the restriction. HOLD as they breathe for a count of 3 and release. Slowly on the exhale back to neutral position. Repeat on both sides.

A scalp massage always feels good!

4. Continue by rocking and shaking the arm. Come down through the hands to clear stagnate energy. Repeat on both sides.

You can combine many techniques in Lomi chair massage! Remember it is your intention and connection that is important.

CHAPTER THIRTY-TWO

WORKING WITH STONES (*PŌHAKU*)

The use of hot stones was common on the islands of Hawai'i. The Hawaiians used everything in nature as a tool, including salts and sticks from branches.

On the island of Hawai'i, you can find the Lomi stone also know as the Keoua Stone, located in the National Park, Pu'uhonua O Hōnaunau. The sun would heat the stone. The client could be laying on the heated stone so that the warmth could penetrate into their muscles and bones while the lomilomi kahuna was doing their healing work.

The Hawaiians might also take a leaf, which contained medicinal qualities and wrap it around a heated stone. The steam that was created would release the medicine from the leaf.

In a modern practice we might use smaller stones on the body. I would highly suggest attending a hot stone course. You will learn how to properly set the temperatures to avoid burning your client and yourself.

Stones need to be energized and cleansed after each use. Sea salt cleansing and placing them back in nature will reenergize your stones.

Stones (hot or cold) also make good tools for deeper pressure.

Be careful with the depth and pressure you use. Never use on bone.

**NEVER place extremely hot stones directly on the skin.
ALWAYS check the temperature on a sensitive part of your skin first.
Check in with your client even if you feel the temperature is ok.**

CHAPTER THIRTY-THREE

CLOSURE

When your lomi session is complete remember to say a gratitude pule for the privilege to have shared your compassionate touch with your client and for all the guidance you have received from the 'Aumakua.

Depending whether you end your session in prone or supine, gently keep your hands connected with your client. As they breathe, lighten the weight of your hands until eventually their exhale detaches from your hand.

I like to use this method as it leaves the client feeling you are still connected with them for a bit longer. It's a less abrupt exit.

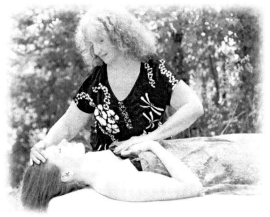

Kumu Karen Carroll shared with me a closing that seals the client in the protection of their ʻAumakua

1. Starting from the crown chakra imagine you are connecting with the rainbow light and lifting out, above and over their body.

2. Bring the Rainbow light all the way to the bottom of their feet.

3. Repeat 3 times using your intention.

Once the client is sealed in the rainbow, stand beside the table in silence.

You are still connected with aka cords (energetic cords). As you perform a clearing for yourself these cords will gently disconnect.

I find that moving at a slower pace away from the table while you are performing your own clearing, gives the client more time to relax and complete their healing process. Most often they do not even realize you have completed the hands on portion of the session and still feel a connection.

CLEARING YOURSELF

There are many methods to clear one self.

1. Prayer
2. Breathing
3. Intention
4. Imagine a waterfall washing over you cleansing and clearing your field of energy. You can do this while using your Hā breath.

Your session is now completed

1. Give your client time to integrate into this world once again.

2. You may want to have some tea, water or a light snack for them.

3. I like to have an extra 15-30 minutes just in case my client feels they need to move slower.

4. Sometimes, emotions may surface and they need to sit with you to process these emotions.

5. Provide a safe space for your client.

6. I like to gift my client with the Hawaiian sarong I used to cover them during the treatment. It is my way of saying Mahalo. Clients love receiving this gift and it reminds them of their wonderful healing session when they are home.

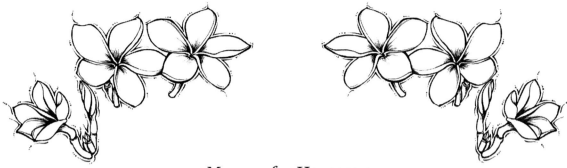

Message for Haumana

You have walked the 'āina and listened to the messages
You have been Maka'ala

You have seen the portals open and received the messages from the 'Aumakua

The salt of Hawai'i has laid upon you and it has fed you

You have received the gifts of Aloha
and learned the skills to gain Lōkahi on your journey

Most importantly you have shared the Hā and the wisdom with the elders
~ Ku'uleialoha

~ *Both Ends of the Rainbow* ~

The rainbow is a symbol to many people. To some it might be the bridge between heaven and earth, the dawn of a new awakening, a sign of good luck, a path for our guides to send messages and a sign a loved one has passed over for some cultures or just the simple expression of beauty in the skies. The rainbow is thought to be an arc although it is truly a circle which some believe represents what is seen and what is unseen. Just as the Hawaiian language has many hidden meanings in their words and deeper meanings, the rainbow can open you to an inner sanctum of exploration of self.

I will now explain why this title was chosen for this book and how the stories I have told weave the healing journey of lomilomi.

Many years ago while I was on a trip driving along the California coastline with my children, their friends and my partner; the rain came pouring down in buckets as the skies were so heavily burdened with clouds. There was no sunshine in sight for hours. I asked my family to set an intention for the sun to come out. The kids chuckled. Within seconds of shifting my consciousness to sunshine, my partner jammed on the brakes and stopped the minivan. There was a vibrant spectrum of colors delicately draped across the skies. Everyone jumped out of the van in awe to witness this colorful display of light from the heavens.

I silently thanked God and in this moment I heard "You will write a book. It will be called *"Both Ends of the Rainbow"*. I was confused and didn't quite understand at that time what this meant. It took nearly 15 years of my journey to come to this point. For years I would start to write and then stop. I knew there was something more, something I had not yet seen or felt or experienced until lomilomi. It was in the land of rainbows, while I lived on Kaua'i, I smiled each day that this message appeared in the sky again. I was reminded that one day I would understand on another level if I remained open and continued to learn. I learned about the Children of the Rainbow, stories by Leinani Melville from the Hawaiian kupuna. Through shared stories I learned that the native Hawaiians believe they were from a place called *Pō*. Now the word *Pō*, like all Hawaiian words, means several things. *Pō* can mean chaos, disorganized, obscure or the celestial realm of God, where man's origins began in a high state of purity or the spirit realm. From *Pō* came the existence of their being. There are other stories of creation you may hear when studying this culture. All are beautiful, fascinating and open one to contemplation of ideas and concepts of creation. Several *kupuna* shared with me that the Hawaiians were star seeds that came from the Pleidian system.

In my own quest on my sacred path, I also had a personal connection with the Egyptian culture and their connection to the Pleiadians. Now you can understand my journey through Egypt was a necessary part of the exploration. I also read Barbara Marciniak's books where she writes about these multidimensional spirit beings. She shares that they were sent to assist humanity with spiritual growth and empowerment. I continued to study about the rainbow connection through the chakra system with Anodea Judith, PhD and Caroline Myss, PhD. This system is the rainbow bridge of our inner sanctuary. All the while, searching for the meaning of both ends of the rainbow, it came one day on a plane. I was looking out the window when a rainbow appeared; the other side of the rainbow. The part that is hidden, the part I never saw before. The circle was complete and the aha moment came over me. I was to search deeper into the hidden meanings. I was to learn that through silence and observation much unfolded information will be shown to me. This reminded me of Nana Veary's life journey and how she explains life comes full circle with a deeper meaning eventually. Nana eventually taught her classes in silence. Students would shift their perspective through listening, observing, feeling and finding the deeper meanings through their own inner exploration. It was in this moment that I was told to create another training, another level. I truthfully had no idea what was to unfold in this new training when I heard the message "If they need to know, they are not ready". The two-year process began as I was guided. I trusted that the students who were ready would show up for the deeper hidden truths and meanings of their life and the hidden meanings of the rainbow connection.

Upon arriving at Half Moon Haven on the sunshine coast of British Columbia, the site of our training, I wondered how all of this would fall into place. There was something very familiar about this region. I had been told there were many sacred grounds and a portal where the Native Indians once resided. I trusted the process and witnessed how it unfolded. A week prior one of my students had asked if I would be able to teach how the stones were used in Lomilomi. To my surprise, the entire beach was covered with stones, just waiting to be ignited. The *pōhaku* (stones) were laughing at me when I noticed them, they were everywhere. There was no doubt in that moment that everything was going to be shown to us if we paid attention. The coincidences were happening moment by moment for everyone. Soon there would be no surprises as we surrendered to everything aligning and being in universal synchrony.

Each morning I realized how easy it was to be present with *ke Akua* and align myself in joy. Messages would wake us in the middle of the night from *ke Akua*, giving us very little sleep. One morning several of us received the same message and found ourselves meeting at the beach. With no words we acknowledged and smiled at each other for we knew we had heard the same message and we just showed up to explore. The tides were low and there before our very eyes was another world, hidden previously to our eyes. Beautiful purple starfish draped

the *pōhaku* like ribbons around a present. The sea sun was a brilliant fluorescent beam of love calling our attention to acknowledge its beauty. The stones were more alive today or maybe we just noticed for the first time. We deliberately stepped with grace paying close attention not to disrupt this amazing world. The energies were intense and we all felt a powerful presence among us. As we walked in grace and reverence with no words spoken we began to hear on another level. The *pōhaku* were excited, like a sea of exuberant three year olds on Christmas morning. They shouted out to us "pick me, pick me, pick me to help heal others".

The *pōhaku* had a potent magnetic energy unlike anything I had previously experienced. I could literally feel the energy in my body being moved and removed. They were happy to be ignited and acknowledged for their purpose. Everyone in the group shared how they could feel the joy from the stones later in the day.

Our days unfolded easily. We cooked together flowing around the kitchen with ease. There was a delightful array of nature's vibrant produce magically and exquisitely prepared with love to nourish our souls. Dancing and singing as we prepared the food together, it seemed more potent and full of energy, it was ineffable. The deep inner stillness we were experiencing was welcomed as it created a more centered space during our training process. Somehow our senses expanded and we connected to the entire universe. Our dreams became more abundant and our reality was shifting quickly. I played witness as I held the space for the group to navigate the unknown. We would notice our thoughts were the same thoughts. Our words became each other's words and the veil was getting thinner as our vibrations were soaring higher each day. One night we slept under the stars on the beach. A deer would frequent and observe our presence. The night grew darker and the fear grew less. A magnificent metamorphosis was evolving before my very eyes. The students had found their purpose. I sat observing these miracles in a humble place. I did not have to do anything for it was already done. No longer did I have to worry or fear how to guide the students. The ownership they were taking was their individual gift. It was emerging and the truth was unfolding as everyone blossomed into their fullness. Love emerged.

The Bowl of Light explains the meaning of *hoʻokuanoʻo*. Kahuna Makua shares the meaning as a meditation that goes with the flow, a vision quest. We were surely experiencing this as our soul was being guided each day. The *ʻAumakua* were waking us early nearly every day to show us our purpose within the greater divine plan. The vision quest is a way for us to deepen our

connection to what is unknown in this reality, as we know it. It is a way to open to the rainbow bridge where the hidden meanings come from our *ʻAumakua*. I knew in every moment not to question a message twice. I was here to facilitate this process for the students. This was their purpose and mission to be here right now.

I recall another message I received, which I did not doubt. "The students" I was told "will participate in an intense breathing session". Magically this unfolded. Our host, Jenn, mentioned there was a local man I should meet. She suggested he might be able to facilitate a breath work session for the students. Well, of course, I thought, it was *the* Divine Plan. The time arrived and the breath work session began. It was in absolute perfect timing, as it should be, the air element. This would open the gateways for the students to remove the blockages holding them back from their next step. As the session began I observed. I could feel and see a shift unfolding for all of us. Everything felt connected. The stones, the sunrise, the tides and our breath, nothing was separate from *ke Akua*. Every cell of our organism became one with each other. I became more aware of a cosmic collective consciousness. I sat by each student as I was randomly guided. I would support and connect as *ke Akua* was advising me. The cries, the screams, the moments of silence as each student found their piece to the whole. This clearing would provide for each of them a new insight to their purpose. Time seemed to stand still and speed up all in the same moment. I cannot explain as this shift was happening so quickly I have no words. I just knew ~ awareness.

The day came for our tandem ocean kayak trek which would be in silence. It was lomilomi in action as the elemental forces would guide us. The element of water would be our teacher. The students had no verbal guidance from me. They did not know what to expect. They trusted and walked to their kayak with confidence and a sense of excitement. We now had a sense of peace and an accelerated sense of self-realization was about to take us through another time warp. As we began to navigate the waters, the tides of life and the lomi connection to it all we seemed to beam through portals of time. We would emerge more fully integrated. Slowly our paddles would move synchronously with our tandem partner. The gentle waves gave us the gentle push we needed that Nana Veary often gave her students. I felt her presence with us.

The ocean became rougher and I had no fear despite I was not an avid swimmer. I stayed calm and trusted this process. I watched the students navigate and work together. It was lomilomi with the water. There were exhilarating moments when we would pause to breathe

together even though no instruction was provided. Our breath would move us through easily. The group of students were supporting each other as our senses became heightened. We navigated through beautiful peaceful coves noticing the inner calm. We observed and witnessed life, our connections and smiled at the glistening silver dollars beneath the clear waters calling out to us "come play". A multitude of sounds sang to us from the waters as our *mana* was gaining more strength. Quickly, we decided to paddle back out to the ocean waves. We looked into each other's eyes, acknowledged our presence together. We took a deep breath and the *mana* soared through all of us. Our lives were changing like the ripples in the water, moving us forward. The stillness around us witnessed our mission. Every gentle breeze on our skin reminded us we are alive.

Then, I stopped paddling as did my tandem partner. I felt something was missing. As I turned to look over my shoulder I noticed our ʻohana was not with us. Silent we waited and prayed. Where had *they* gone? Where had *we* gone? Time seemed to be moving very slowly again. I began to breathe more deeply with my lomi partner. Energetically I called out to find our ʻohana. Still there was silence as we waited in this vast ocean. I turned around again to see an exquisite rock formation I had not noticed just moments ago. Something was peeking around this *pōhaku* when suddenly a powerful warrior goddess emerged. A kayak deliberately and smoothly floating led by Jenn moved through the strong current. She sat upright like a Viking Queen and we were once again connected. All the paddlers stopped. We watched not from our eyes this time. The kayaks seemed to navigate us with no human direction safely back to the shore as we merely observed the vibrant greens reflecting upon the ocean water. There was a thread of light, I could see, connecting all of us as we arrived safely back to the shore…*together*. There would be no separateness from us from this point on. The group shared later that night that this was the pivotal point of their personal transformation. We had witnessed the miracle of the element of water. Our focus became more intentional as we learned about *pono* in our reality and in relationship to each other. We found the simplicity that existed in our *uhane* (Spirit Perfected). The subconscious wounds and scars that we may have held onto were releasing with the simple *Hā* breath. We waited for *makana* (the gift). A greater understanding of walking in both worlds, that which is seen and unseen was now showing us how to open to limitless possibilities. It was becoming easier to navigate both ends of the rainbow.

That evening we gathered around a fire at the beach. We prayed together. With our *Hā* breath we set our intentions to write a new chapter in our book of life. The power of thoughts, the spoken word, the breath we shared along with the energy of joy we would manifest our new life. The ʻohana was excited for each other as we shared our stories. Then we would take our breath and blow it into the fire witnessing the flame get larger and stronger. The ʻohana was excited for each new story because we knew that this elemental force would ignite our desire. That night we would all sleep soundly. The ʻAumakua would not wake us up early. Our work was done for now.

When we embraced this new paradigm and realized we were not alone everything aligned itself in right divine order. All we had to do was show up joyously and receive. There were no words specifically for this journey; we just seemed to know we would never be the same. Within each set of eyes I saw myself, a beautiful reflection of spirit immersed in the grace of Love.

This vision quest, this meditation in movement allowed for our frequency to rise higher during our final exchange of lomilomi. The love flowed effortlessly. The ʻAumakua and *pōhaku* supported every moment loving us. Healing was happening on all levels as the physical bodies lay peacefully in transition through time and space. We connected with *Both Ends of the Rainbow*.

This is lomilomi ~

The life path of giving, receiving and knowing your purpose.

It is the living lomi that flows through our divine heart and where we can find peace.

It is this living lomi that will show you the deeper meaning, the hidden messages and the circle of life. It is the path to our 'Aumakua when you listen and trust. Where the knowledge and wisdom can be shared. It is Both Ends of the Rainbow.

We have awakened
There is nothing more I can say
For there are no words
Only an experience
A miracle, when we allow the full spectrum to be revealed from
Both Ends of the Rainbow

Haumana Stories

~ *Jena Rowland* ~

I had no idea what was in store for me when I signed up for this class. I was feeling stuck, both in my personal life and in my professional life. I felt this weight and worn out and stuck within the same routines unable to break away. Well, the first three days of the intensive class was pure healing for me. From emotional releases to working through deeply rooted issues, Lomi gave me exactly what I needed. It provides that sacred space both emotionally and physically, so that you can fully heal in a nurturing, supportive environment. Lomi allows you to release those things that are weighing you down. It teaches you to let go. It was that missing piece to the healing puzzle. By the time the intensive class was over, I felt like a new person. I was lighter and positively glowing, and I still am. The lessons I learned from Lomi Lomi not only changed me, but it changed my life, my outlook and my perspective. It carried over into my massage business, not only as I worked on clients, but in the way I worked. It brought back that spiritual aspect of healing and renewed my passion for massage & healing. As a Reiki Master I often incorporated energy work into my sessions, but it was limited. Lomi taught me to strip away labels and limitations. Energy is limitless and boundless, so our energy work should be to. Despite having already taught Reiki I was clearly guided to rewrite my Reiki courses with this in mind and thus my book on Shamanic Reiki Therapy Tradition was born. In my 10 years as a massage therapist, I have never come across a class that provided so much on so many different levels and I am forever grateful to have learned this sacred healing.

Jena Rowland, NC LMBT#6986

~ Mende Garren ~

When I walked through the front doors of the Bend of Ivy Lodge in 2007, I thought the week of training I was going to experience would simply earn me some CE's and teach me some new techniques. I had no idea that this class would change my life. Back then, I held on to everything; both physical and emotional. I was weighed down and mentally exhausted. It was fitting that the lesson I attracted that week was "Letting Go". I still vividly remember my healing session, with me crying hysterically on the floor while my Lomi family attentively supported me. Gloria sat at my head and told me it was okay to acknowledge my feelings. I let go of many emotional pains that week but had no idea that it had just scratched the surface. I left behind the shroud of darkness that had suffocated me for so long.

Almost 6 years later, I am truly a new person. I am able to let go of things that I allowed to leech onto me and hook into me. I have replaced feelings of frustration and anger with feelings of happiness and love. I share this love with those around me. I aspire to become a better person because I know that I am love. It is my nature to love those around me and to accept their love in return. I am worth loving.

Lomi has changed my whole perspective as a massage therapist when it comes to giving massage. I now hold a space with each client and intuitively listen to their needs. I am not afraid to pause for a moment to perform energy work to a client. I no longer fear the client popping an eye open and asking why I stopped moving. Overall, I have peace of mind that I had not experienced before learning Lomi.

I am so thankful that Gloria is in my life. Had she not listened to her calling, I might still be living in darkness.

~ *Kat Damron* ~

Expressions of Spirit

All knew what happened. We were there, awake and aware.

There was a warm presence brought on by the wind
Whispers and Chants could be heard, but what was said?
No one was sure.

We battled as it twisted itself inside of us.
A red hot rage came over, then the push stopped and we began to breathe.

This was like watching the earth embrace the first human form at birth.
The first moment the lips of the closest star kissed the atmosphere.
It was raw love.

In that space, void of time, we accepted that we knew nothing
and opened to spirit to receive anything.
All was love and love was all.

Many things were taught by spirit.
The quiet tone that was set allowed everyone to acquire the wisdom
desired by themselves.

We learned to listen to our inner voices and each other.
We owned our intentsion and were hypnotized by the truth.

A divine being crossed our paths that day.
No name was given, no words spoken.
We were there, awake and aware.

~ *Daniel LaCroix* ~

First I want to say thank you for your guiding and mentoring Kumu Gloria. After my five days of Lomi Lomi training, I knew that a shift had happen. I didn't know where it would take me. I still do not know, no one knows. That is the beauty of it all. Going to the advanced retreat in Vancouver was not an easy preparation. I encountered many obstacles. I almost cancelled at one point. However, the power of prayer; the mentoring group I have participated in for the last year; listening to the spirit and trusting the journey; allowed me to live this journey with no expectations. That is when healing, wisdom happens.

I knew that it was not going to be a class with techniques and was very blessed to find out that it was a journey for me, to go deeper in finding my purpose, who I am and why I am here.

We spent long hours in silence, the teaching of Kumu, the beautiful spiritual place, the amazing love and caring, the wonderful food. All was there to allow me to trust, to let go, to feel, to be vulnerable in the moment.

I am not going to write every detail of my journey, as it would take a lot of writing. I will share the miracle of this experience. It took me months to realize the power of the work we all experienced.

The messages came one after another at anytime of the night.

Kumu told us to not go back to sleep but listen, get up, trust and do the work. Each night I woke, I even felt a bear sniffing me one evening when I decided to sleep on the beach. I felt safe, loved, one with the spirit, my ʻohana , nature, and in lōkahi. Each day brought more surprises to my soul.

I am a man who was hurt by other men. Trusting men has been a real challenge. The company of women's souls is always so easy. My journey brought me in front of my fear of men. Yet this calling, a mission to teach men to open the sweet, soft feminine side of their being allowed me to truly accept being grounded on earth. I was told that I am to learn about earth medicine, plants, oil and much more. I became aware, like never before, of how much spirit is with me, guides me and trusts me. And yet it is still hard sometimes to believe it and to be totally vulnerable and know that I am enough.

When I went back home to St. Louis, I went back into my world. I was still in such a place of high vibration and noticed a much lower vibration from other people and places. It took me a long time to reintegrate and it was quite a challenge to keep this beautiful experience alive.

Almost four months have passed by and out of nowhere the shift happened. Souls came in my life with messages. I found myself confused, in pain, as I thought that I was going in one direction and suddenly I was sent on a path I did not expect.

I was told that I had to learn so much. It was time to come back home - my home with Jesus. I was confused as I learned so much from the indigenous world and the Hawaiian culture. Then the message came stronger and stronger and I surrendered. I let myself become vulnerable and listen. I know today that my learning of Lomi and the Hawaiian culture is not over as well as learning about many other traditions. I know that I am following spirit and being guided to study plants and oils. I know that if it was not for my journey to Lomilomi and the advanced training with the teaching of the ancestors and Kumu, I would not have listened to the call to come back home with Jesus.

My faith has never been so strong. My thirst to learn, discover, share, teach and be of service to the world and humanity is present each and everyday.

I am so blessed to have the support of my amazing wife Melisa. She is so loving and supportive. I am so blessed to have Kumu, my 'Ohana, my church, my group Invitation to Life and the guidance of Jesus, Mary, my teacher Yvonne and many spirits and ancestors.

I used to say, "Why me"? Now I can say, "Why not me"? I am Daniel, just another soul on this amazing planet, here to be of service to humanity wherever the spirit needs me. "I am enough".

~ Daniel

~ *Sarah Bordeau-Rigterink* ~

To walk between two worlds
while fire burns a flesh born child
of the Galaxies
Billowing air may breathe life more completely
fanning the flames riding the waves
of eternity
within the grounding confines
of Universe
Dirt and wood grasping at mortal being
an immortal soul exits
rational thought
to dig deeper into Earthbody
seeking answers to questions
only images may ask
and only forever can keep

We all have quirky little habits, tendencies or fears that seem to have come from nowhere. I started on this path at a young age. Before the vision quest I felt unworthy of my gifts, and therefore held myself back, hindering myself from reaching my full potential. I denied my ability to walk consciously between worlds, choosing instead to wander in physical and spirit world without appropriate awareness. Though having experienced many loved ones crossing, I clung to my fear of death like iron to a magnetic pendulum; in some instances I have felt completely at ease with my mortality, and other times I panicked, clinging to denial. As we lay down to breathe, my greatest fears surfaced quickly. As the visions started I was shown many past lives in great color and detail. I watched myself dancing in ecstasy around a family fire. In trance, the heat from within my body burned until I fell into the flames; though it cooled my spirit body, the fire still burned my flesh. I saw myself in a city numbing myself with needles until I finally succumbed to the fear, dying because I ran away from the sensitivity that was too much for me to bear. While I witnessed these things, I felt the heat in my soul greater than any fire that burns. I felt the chill of death when time after time my ancient knowledge failed or suffocated me, until my body could take no more. And I laughed. I laughed with the knowledge that the wisdom is always with me. I laughed because my fear of feeling has already been faced and conquered and faced again. And while I still traveled to faraway destinations and times, a calm came over me. All the knowledge I was afraid I couldn't possibly have, at only 24, came with a simple breath. The fire and cold moved through me with every inhalation, and answers coming from a place larger than me, to questions I have worried over for so long, coursed through me with every exhalation. I realized that all I need is faith to allow the divine mystery to inspire me, and awareness of breath to lead me through any darkness that I may encounter. Once the vision quest was over, I realized that I had very easily been aware of my earthly body, as well as the experiences that my spirit needed me to become conscious of. And I was still breathing!

When I gather with others within the intention of raising our vibration, and that of all the planet, there are flashes where we become divinity. I have brief moments like this when in meditation and with healees, however when a potent group of people get together on sacred land with sacred purpose those moments become whole chunks of time. This is where I see my greatest potential, and this vision quest was one of those opportunities. It becomes easy to create a bubble among my peers, and the challenge is always to integrate new knowledge into the mundane miracles of every day existence. Luckily, there is no way for me to unlearn this experience. There are challenges that have come up that seem to test precisely what I learned about myself during the quest. I am closer to living within my full potency every day, and find myself navigating through life more fluidly. I am still working toward the full potential I experienced during the vision quest, yet now I acknowledge that I am choosing to slowly accept my potency at a rate that feels right. I am more aware of my fears before I start dictating my life by them, and more easily observe and work through them with enhanced compassion for myself. I am moving as quickly as the slowest part of me needs to go (and sometimes a few steps faster), enabling myself to stand more comfortably within my full power while doing so. I have learned that, while challenges will continually arise, by breathing deeply I can center myself in my true nature creating more options, perspectives and opportunities in doing so. I am truly grateful for every chance to own my potency more fully, and the vision quest exposed me to what potential is possible. I eagerly anticipate looking back at where I am today with wonder, and am open to what great mysteries lay ahead!

~ *Jenn Fletcher* ~

My quest with Aloha began simply enough...

A friend offered a Lomi Lomi session to me.

"A what session?" I asked....having no idea what the offer actually was.

"Hawaiian Lomi Lomi massage" he said, with a little twinkle in his eye, like he quietly knew something potent, of which I was now intrigued. He briefly explained it to me, although I wasn't so much interested in the details, just the feeling that was behind them, and if what he spoke of could bring relief to my 6 ft frame and achy muscles. Ever since I'd had a nasty car accident when I was younger, I loved massage, and was familiar with its benefits and the relaxation it could bring.

As he spoke about it, I felt beyond his words, still struck by a sense of something both familiar, and something I had not yet been privy to , like there was an ancient world behind what he was offering. There was also a quality of confidence and laughter with his generous gesture...free of any attachment as to whether I accepted, or not.

The offer had come from the heart.

Having only had swedish massage in the past, nothing could have prepared me for the experience I was about to have, something which far transcended any massage, but rather, would take me into an alternate experience of reality.

Arriving to the treatment space, I was a bit nervous.

Despite loving bodywork, I always was a bit hesitant with people touching my body...my own self consciousness arising in my 20 something self.

Being highly sensitive to energy since birth (although never realizing it, or even thinking of it like that)... I felt the nervousness in my belly.

The wisdom of my body knew something was up!~

Once face down on the table, a sheet covering me....my practitioner friend began to chant a prayer, of which I didn't understand or expect. My mind wanted to know what it meant, what was going to happen next, it wanted to understand everything!

He kept on with the Hawaiian chant, as he began moving around the table in some kind of a dance that started activating more than just my mind.

It was overwhelming at first, even knowing this person, and I let my mind take control for a moment.

As he danced around in what I now know as "The Flight", a powerful dance that is profound for activating the body, the breath, and connecting one to Source....I became increasingly aware and interested in what was happening within me. He hadn't touched me physically, and yet I could already feel tingling in my fingers, and movement in my cells, like someone was stirring the pot that was the container of my being.

Once the dance was done, and the flowing strokes of mindful massage began, my breath deepened, my body starting to decompress, as the layers and layers of things I had unconsciously been holding, suppressing, shoving down or denying, began to surface.

The feelings I had been unwilling to feel began to flow, as I became more and more willing to feel them and let them go.

Parts of my body that had become numb to full functioning and vitality were renewed.... the muscles releasing their calcified negative patterns in the cellular memory, patterns that no longer supported me.

Visions and images appeared before me, Native elders, swirls of a traditional pipe, white buffalo, a tribe long forgotten.

Pictures I was not intending to see or trying to conjure revealed themselves to me, one after another, even beyond my understanding of their significance or meaning. I began hearing old native chants, and felt waves of wisdom being whispered to my subconscious mind by those invisible to touch... stored for a later time when I could absorb and translate these gifts to life.

Memories of past lives, of times before when tribes were One, and ways were simple were remembered, and a deeper calling that still is working me now as I write were unravelled. An eternity of life was explored.

It was time to flip over.

In the place I had just been, I had forgotten my body even existed. My mind was so completely disengaged that it seemed like a task to even comprehend having a body, let alone moving its heavy jelly like container from its current position.

What felt like an eternity had been only over an hour, and as I was helped to a sitting, and eventually a standing position to visit the bathroom, I felt like I was a small child, new to this world, to this body, to everything that was around me, as if my eyes were only experiencing physical reality for the first time.

Everything was glowing, radiating slightly, like it had all been illuminated by a gentle glow, each with various colours.

And still there was the mundane tasks that we take for granted.

Going to the bathroom was a whole experience in and of itself. Suddenly I was keenly aware of my entire kidney system (of all the systems of my body actually), that ran throughout the entire portion of my body.

THIS was MY body?!? Really?!!

It had NEVER felt like THIS before!

Woah! I thought to myself, trying to comprehend this new state.

What was happening? What had already happened?

(Again the ego mind kicking in for just a second to try to understand).

Within only a few seconds of trying to think though, it became too much effort, and I surrendered back to the massage table, and the experience that was only half over! I had only just touched the surface!

Its been over 10 years since that experience.

As I write this now, I have had the absolute honour and pleasure of receiving many hours of Hawaiian Lomi Lomi Massage, both Traditional and Temple style.

Its been 5 years that I have been studying this Art form myself, always learning, growing, transforming and falling into deeper reverence and gratitude for the profound gifts that have come. After hundreds of hours of training, and facilitating well over 1000 hours of massage it is apparently clear that I have still only touched the surface of this Infinitely graceful way of healing and living.

Mahalo and Aloha

Jennifer Fletcher

Leilani Eagle Medicine Woman

www.halfmoonhaven.com

~ *Candy "Kainoa" Thomen* ~

As Kumu Gloria Ku'uleialoha said at the beginning of the book, Lomilomi found me. It called me and I answered. I answered without having any clear idea about what I was doing or why. I answered the call without knowing the profound effect it would have on my entire being, my whole life and my way of living, my whole concept of the Universe as I knew it then.

Lomilomi has changed me. It has helped me to begin the process of Awakening. Lomilomi has brought me to a place that I did not know existed. I always dreamed that it did, but I had no knowledge of how to get here or to even know that it was truly real. And I have only begun to know the depth of that which I do not know.

Lomilomi for me is a Journey into listening, into silence, into that deep inner-knowing place that connects us with all that is, was, and ever shall be. It has been a path of discovering my inner quiet and thereto my outer quiet. It is a Journey towards and into Peace, Love and Compassion and through those, Healing.

The changes in my Self and my life have been astonishing since my Lomi journey began. I truly am not the person I was in 2011 and I am so blessed and grateful. Who I was then was exactly who I needed to be at that time. Who I am now is a beautiful unfolding of that person, that seed-being that I was. Now I am the blossom, the bud of the flower starting to open to the sun.

ADVANCED TRAINING RETREAT - BRITISH COLUMBIA

At the end of my first Kaua'i retreat in 2011, Kumu mentioned the possibility of an Advanced Lomi Training Retreat and I immediately knew that I was going to go, that I had to be there. I felt called, compelled to go once again.

As with all birth processes and new beginnings, my Journey has not been all sunshine and roses. I have fought, kicked and screamed, beat my fists on the ground, thrown temper tantrums to beat all temper tantrums and more than a few times have planted my butt firmly in the sand and flat refused to go any further on my Spiritual quest. I have shaken my fists at the sky. I have also prayed, and given thanks and so much love to this Journey. As with all things, it goes in waves. I fought hard at the first retreat and Kumu told me many times that none of this has to be hard. WE make it hard or easy, it's entirely up to us.

Despite being in a really good place in my Journey, during the months leading up to the Advanced Training in British Columbia, I started fighting once again (although I didn't realize at the time that's what I was doing). There were also massive life-altering changes happening in my world. I began to create reasons not to go to BC – I wasn't unpacked from moving, I didn't have the money, I didn't have the time, I didn't want to be away from my boyfriend. But I needed to go and *ke Akua* moved me, step by step, forward on my Path.

It was a 12-hour drive to beautiful Sechelt, British Columbia. Nature called out to me in a joyful voice. In the haze of one of my biggest spiritual temper tantrums ever, I tried to ignore her beautiful voice. The closer we got to the retreat, the angrier I got. Angry at nothing, angry at everything. What was really going on is that I was terrified of what was going to happen at this retreat. I knew deep down the massive shifts that had occurred in Kaua'i and I was petrified of what was going to shift this time.

The retreat center was amazingly beautiful, with the ocean and the beach just steps out the back door. Ancient trees surrounded us, breathtaking beauty and peace was everywhere, the gentle voices of the *'aumakua* whispered all around me. And I was pissed off!

On our first night, after dinner, we took turns sharing our reasons for being there. I honestly don't remember what I said that night. I remember it being hard to say and I cried a lot and fought to even get the words out. After I said what I could say, Kumu looked me straight in the eye and said "Give me your keys." My heart stopped. For me, this was the most potent symbol she could have asked for. In my mind, it was my very freedom that she was asking me to hand over. What it truly represented was my ability to run away. With every ounce of strength that I could muster, I stood up, walked into my room, got the keys to my truck and took them back to her. You would think this was my surrender, my act of compliance to acknowledge what I was there to do. But it was just the beginning.

As we all sat around the table, Kumu shared what she had been guided to do during this retreat. We were given the task of creating a Vision Quest for ourselves to encompass the next 5 days. She told us we were to be open to our Guides, the *'aumakua* and *ke Akua* and to truly listen. And we were asked "What would you do to honor your Quest?"

I decided that my Vision Quest was to find out, once and for all, what I was here to do. What was my purpose for being here on this planet at this time? This question had been chasing me and causing more spiritual temper tantrums than any other. Little did I know that the true Vision Quest was to find out WHO AM I. Because in learning who we are, the answer to why we are here is made clear.

Even in the midst of my turmoil, powerful things were happening, shifts were already occurring. We participated in a powerful breath work session. Each individual experience was beautiful and powerful. For me, the *'aumakua* of the place we were in made themselves known to me in spirit and in form. They shared their Spirit with me, embraced me and showed me pieces of myself. I was given so many gift s during that session. Again, one would think this was the breakthrough moment. But no, I was still fighting. Even in the midst of receiving the gifts I was given, I was still fighting as hard as I possibly could.

As a group we attended a dinner event at a local restaurant. My anger was palpable and I had barriers up higher and thicker than the Great Wall. I sometimes feel guilty for subjecting my 'ohana to all of this, but I also know that everything happens for a reason and my anger and resistance had its reasons for everyone. Lessons are learned at levels we sometimes aren't even aware of and from things that we wouldn't expect.

The next day went much the same as the previous days. That night after dinner, Kumu said "we need to check in and see where we're at." Oh lord, I thought. This was the last thing I wanted to do. Again we went around the table, each person sharing where they were at. Then it came to me. I honestly contemplated lying about where I was at. As bad as that sounds, I thought I might get away with it and not have to face where I was at and what I was doing. But instead I chose to honor what I have been taught by Kumu about being *pono* and to honor her and my *'ohana* with the truth, as hard as it was to speak. So I laid it all out. "I don't want to be here." I spoke my truth all the way down to the bottom of what I was feeling. I didn't want to be in BC, I didn't want to go to Kaua'i three weeks later to be a part of my second residential retreat, I didn't want to be a part of any of it. There was a lot more including massive doubts about myself, my Journey.

As those who were sharing this space and this time with me absorbed what I was saying, one of the women attending looked at me across the table and said "I feel that we need to tell you one thing that we appreciate about you. And you need to sit there and take it in. Feel it, absorb it, accept it and make it part of you." I was terrified. I looked at Kumu and begged her with my eyes to not make me do this. Begged!!!! And she looked at me with her knowing, beautiful eyes and said, "You can make this hard or you can make this easy. It's your choice. Trust me, this is the easy way."

And THIS is when the miracle occured and the shift happened. One by one my *'ohana* looked me straight in the eye and shared on thing they appreciated about me. I breathed it in, I accepted it, I held it and embraced it and I shifted. For me, this moment was lomilomi at its very essence and not one hand touched me. It was LOVE. My heart opened, my barriers came down, and my highest self came to the forefront once again. I stepped back into my *self* and was welcomed with love and open arms. It was one of the most powerful experiences I have ever had and I've had quite a few since this journey started. This was pure Love, pure Spirit coming into our presence and shifting my resistance to acceptance, lifting my fear and removing my doubt.

The next few days were time out of time. I communed with the 'āina and the 'aumakua in a way that was utterly profound. I heard the 'aumakua speak through the trees, the stones, the wind, in the voices of the star fish and two beautiful sea suns. Through the herons, the ravens, through everything that surrounded me. I opened the eyes and ears of my heart and knowledge was there for me. I slept outside and heard the stars in their joy begging me to look at them, to admire their beauty, when all I wanted to do was sleep. I heard the joyful, child-like voices of the stones as we asked and then chose them to heal through stone massage. I heard and felt the Spirit of the great protector tree that stood at the doorway to the yurt where we practiced. And I shared deeply with my 'ohana and with our Kumu on a level that was pure love.

The retreat was powerful beyond words. It was beautiful and so much was given to me. I learned at the deepest level so much about who I am and what I am capable of. And one of the most important things I learned is that it doesn't have to be hard. When we finally stop fighting, when we release our fear and our self-doubt, when we are truly ready to receive, it is a beautiful, joyful, easy experience that transcends all else.

I came home from those five days in a completely new space, a space of deep and profound Peace. As I lay in bed with my husband that first night, sharing the journey with him, he said one of the most profound things I've heard. He said "Honey, you did not leave and go to that retreat. But I got YOU back." And he was right. I had once again found my deepest, truest self. I had been unaware of being hidden again, buried under the stress of the changes I had been going through. But once I was met with and passed through the barrier of what I had become, I found myself once again. I am grateful.

There is so much that lomilomi is and so much that cannot be put into words. I am eternally grateful to have found this path and to be embarking upon this Journey. It has brought me to places that I never dreamed existed. And I know that it has only just begun.

~ Candy "Kainoa" Thomen

P.S. I DID go to Kaua'i three weeks later and it was yet another powerful, amazing Journey.

PELE'S DREAM
Pele's gift to Gloria in a dream

They have forgotten of the ways of old
When there was balance and ancient teachings were told
It is time for all of us to see
That the old ways of our earth, are a necessity

They have forgotten
To show reverence each day and there is sadness in my soul, I regret to say.
So now, I call upon you dear ones, to teach the children the ways

As we learn to flow in harmony with all that we create
I will hold you dear….. in my heart each day
For there was a time when all was simple, you see and
The colors of the rainbow were our eternity

So learn the ways of Pono and open your heart
Share Aloha, in everything you do
Wipe my tears away from my aging face,
I beg of you…. to…
Teach Aloha….
Bring unity to our place….

Teach Aloha I ask of you today
So the children may have the strength and grace,
to Teach Aloha to the future of our race.

So listen to me now, as our planet goes through rebirth….
There will be times when we question the gods
so
Teach Aloha, please….. and you will see
There is greatness and peace in harmony

So I tell you once more, the time is now!
Wash away the pain and let it go to sea.
Breathe deeply into the life that awaits perfect harmony….. and live

Aloooohaaaa~ Ahhhhhlohaaaa!
~Aloha~

PELE'S DREAM
Pele's gift to Gloria in a dream

Original oil painting by Ku'uleialoha

Live Aloha

A – Akahai

Kindness, to be expressed with tenderness

L – Lokahai

Unity, to be expressed with harmony

O – 'Olu'olu

Agreeable, to be expressed with pleasantness

H – Ha'aha'a

Humility, to be expressed with modesty

A – Ahonui

Patience, to be expressed with perseverance

Mahalo

Ku'uleialoha

Pronouncing Hawaiian Words

The Hawaiian language consists mostly of vowel sounds. The spoken sounds were translated into 12 letters.

Vowels : a e i o u

Consonants: h k l m n p w

You will find several symbols that will change the pronunciation, which is very critical in their language.

Double vowels are separated with an ʻ*okina* (which looks similar to an apostrophe)

For example: aʻo

The W is often pronounced like ʻVee" as in Hawaiʻi.

For many years after the missionaries invaded the Hawaiian islands, they were not allowed to speak their own language. Today, the Hawaiian language is being taught in schools once again.

Let's try these sounds

a = as in papa

e = as in hey (a)

i = as in eat

o = as in oval

u = as in you

The vowels give *oli*, the chant power. The *Kanaka Maoli* use active verbals forms in their *pule*, repeating chants and creating a mesmerizing or hypnotic state of being.

Glossary of Hawaiian Words

ʻāina	land, nature, mother earth
aka cord	an invisible connection with others or things
Akua (ke Akua)	God, Source, Great Spirit
aloha	Compassion, love, friendship, the spirit and breath of Akua
ʻalaea	(water-soluble colloidal orcherous earth, used for medicine, dyes, special ceremonies)
ʻāmama	closing of a prayer
ʻaumakua	guardian, spirit, ancestors, source
ʻAumakua	our deceased loved ones, spirits
hā	to breathe, exhale, the breath of life, the number four
haʻahaʻa	humility
hale	house or building
halāu	school
haole	non-Hawaiian, one without spirit, a foreigner
haumana	students
heiau	temple, sacred site, religious structure, pre Christian place of worship
hoʻoponopono	The art of forgiveness and making it right, reconciliation, to make better
hui	together; club/group/association; to join/unite
hula	Hawaiian traditional dance
ʻimoʻimo	sparkle, as in the eye
kaʻaleleau	flying, a style of lua or martial arts, movement
kahu	priest, care taker, one who holds the wisdom of their geneology
kahuna	Master, Hawaiian priest, keeper of secrets or knowledge, minister, expert
kala	forgiveness, freedom, release, free; to loosen, release, forgive
kalo	taro, the staple crop for hawaiʻi
kanaka	man; human being; plural is kānaka
kanaka maoli	Native Hawaiians, "real man" is a literal translation

kāne	man
kapu	forbidden
kealaola	pathway to healing
keiki	children
kekahi i kekahi	one by one; each and every one
koa	courage; brave/courageous; warrior; hardwood tree
kumu	teacher; base foundation
kuleana	responsibility
kupuna	elders; (plural is kūpuna)
lā'au lapa'au	herbal medicine, medicine
laulima	working with hands, working together
lōkahi	Balance, Harmony, Unity
lomi	a term to describe massage, also described as a shift of energy, a way of life
lua	type of Hawaiian Martial arts; cellar/bathroom
mana	spiritual power, divine power
makuahine	mother, aunt, female cousin
mauli ola	source of life
mea'ai pono	balanced nutrition
mele	song
na'auao	wisdom
'ohana	family, extended family, universal family, clan
ola	life, health , well being
oli	chant
opu lomi	stomach massage
pa'akai	sea salt or salt
piko	connections points, umbilical, crown of head
pilikia	trauma, drama, troubles
pō	night, chaos
pōhaku	stones
poi	a staple food of the islands made from the kalo; the Hawaiian staff of life, made from cooked taro corms
pono	all that is righteous, balanced, goodness, fair
pule	prayer
pu'uwai	heart center, emotions
wahine	woman

Bibliography

Chai, R Makana Risser. Na Mo'olelo Lomilomi, The traditions of Hawaiian massage and healing. 2005 by the Bishop Museum. ISBN # 1-58178-046-X

Chai, R Makana Risser. Hawaiian Massage * Lomilomi Sacred Touch of Aloha. 2007 by Hawaiian Insights. ISBN 978-0-9791867-0-7

Hrehorczak-Stephens, Tamara. Abraham Kawai'i, a brief history of the man, the kahuna and kahuna bodywork. 2012 Create space publishing platform ISBN 1479333255, 978-1479333257

Jim, Harry Uhane and Garnette Arledge. Wise Secrets of Aloha, Learn and live the Sacred art of Lomilomi. 2007. ISBN# 1-57863-398-2

Kahalewai, Nancy S. Hawaiian Lomilomi, Big Island Massage. 2004 ISBN # 0-9677253-2-1

Kahn, Elithe Manuha'aipo, PhD. Hā Breathe! 2004 by Zen Care. ISBN 978-0-9747334-1-8

Lee, Pali J and John Koko Willis. Ho'opono. ISBN 978-09677253-7-6 (out of print)

Lee, Pali J and John Koko Willis. Tales From the Night Rainbow. 1990 ISBN # 0-9628030-0-6

Melville, Leinani. Children of the Rainbow, The religion, legends and gods of pre-Christian Hawai'i. 1969 ISBN # 0-8356-0002-5

Pukui, Mary Kawena and Samuel H Elbert. New Pocket Hawaiian Dictionary. University of Hawai'I Press, 1992 ISBN# 0-8248-1392-8

Veary, Nana. Change We Must, my spiritual journey. 1989 Published by the Institute of Zen Studies (out of print) ISBN # 1-877982-07-5

Wesselman, Hank. The Bowl of Light, Ancestral Wisdom from a Hawaiian Shaman. 2011 ISBN # 978-1-60407-455-0

Resources

Lomilomi Trainings Offered by Ku'uleialoha
On the mainland and Kaua'i
Visit www.Lomilomimassagece.com

Order copies of Both Ends of the Rainbow, Aloha Messages card decks and the vibrant and colorful giclee on canvas prints of Pele's Dream.

www.GloriaCoppola.com

Trainings by our contributing Kumu

S. Pualani Gillespie	www.Lomilomitraditions.com
Kumu Karen Leialoha Carroll	www.kapuaokalani.com
Angeline's Kauai Lomi Lomi Massage	www.angelineslomikauai.com
Kumu Dane Kaohelani Silva	http://haleola.com
Kumu Brenda Mohalapua Ignacio	www.lomilomialoha.com
Kumu Penny Prior	www.hawaiianmassage.com
Kumu Harry Uhane Jim	www.harryjimlomilomi.com

More trainings

Maka'ala Yates - Mana Lomi®	www.manalomi.com
Barbara Helynn	www.lomilomi-massage.org
Jairo Kealoha Cardona	www.sacredbodywork.us
Tom Cochran and Donna Jason	www.sacredlomi.com
Wayne Kealohi Powell	www.shamanicbodywork.com

Credits

Visio Photography - James and Jen Tarpley

Models   Kellie Grindstaff; Brittany Brinkley; Linda Balich

Hawaii photos and others taken by Gloria Coppola and students, reproduced with permission.

Cover Design, Book Layout and original plumeria illustration - Candy Kainoa Thomen Seraphim Healing Art ~ Original artwork for healing. Graphic design for healers and the healing profession by a healer. - www.SeraphimHealingArt.com

CPSIA information can be obtained at www.ICGtesting.com
Printed in the USA
BVOW05s0144200114

342427BV00001B/18/P